"If There Were Any Victims…"

An inside look into the El Mirage, Arizona child sex crimes cases mishandled by Maricopa County Sheriff Joe Arpaio's Office.

A book by Bill Louis

The information contained in this book is based on the author's personal experience, training and research. Reasonable, good-faith efforts were made to provide reliable and accurate information. The names and addresses of the victims, witnesses and suspects in the 31 police reports have been changed to protect their privacy. Other literary steps were taken to avoid jeopardizing the investigation or prosecution of those criminal cases.

Reality Writing
8380 W. Emile Zola Avenue
Suite #5861
Peoria, Arizona 85381

Reality Writing, L.L.C., 8380 W. Emile Zola Avenue, Suite # 5861
Peoria, Arizona 85381

Visit our Web site at www.realitywritingllc.com

Printed in the United States of America

ISBN: 978-0-9855912-0-5

First printing: May 2012

This book is dedicated to my family - who supported me throughout my military and law enforcement careers.

.

Table of Contents

Prologue

by Bill Louis

In late 2011, Associated Press reporter Jacques Billeaud wrote an article exposing serious negligence over hundreds of sex crimes cases that Maricopa County (Arizona) Sheriff Joe Arpaio's office failed to properly investigate.

This wasn't the first news article to showcase the sheriff's bungling of these crimes. Ryan Gabrielson, a writer for the *The East Valley Tribune* (Mesa, Arizona) was awarded a Pulitzer Prize for an in-depth article in 2008 on the mishandling of these cases. Lisa Halverstadt with the *Arizona Republic* wrote several articles in 2008/2009 focusing specifically on the dozens of El Mirage, Arizona sex-crime cases that Arpaio's detectives neglected or failed to investigate.

In November 2007 the new police chief of the El Mirage Police Department informed Arpaio's office they had discovered dozens of serious crime cases that his detectives didn't investigate properly - or at all.

Billeaud interviewed me several times in the weeks preceding his article in December 2011. I provided him with factual information about the cases that Arpaio's office had bungled in El Mirage. The article gave the reading public a snapshot of the negligence the sheriff's office was now facing over the mishandling of hundreds of sex crimes — many including child victims. Most of the cases had been mishandled or just completely ignored.

The Associated Press *exposé* set off a fire storm of local and national negativity against the Arizona sheriff. Scores of print media articles, editorials and blogs were written over the next few days in major newspapers across the United States. The entire scandalous incident was an embarrassment to the Arizona law man who routinely described himself as "America's Toughest Sheriff."

On Monday, December 5, 2011 Sheriff Arpaio held a live press conference with his Chief Deputy to respond to the allegations revealed in the AP report. During the press conference Arpaio issued an "apology" to the victims of the cases his office had botched or failed to investigate.

As I watched the press conference on television I wondered how "Sheriff Joe" was going to handle himself. Perhaps this was to be the press conference where Sheriff

Arpaio was going to do the right thing and accept responsibility.

And then Joe Arpaio started talking. In his typical condescending tone he said, *"If there were any victims out there I apologize to those victims - if there were any."*

If there were any victims?? If there was <u>anyone</u> in all of Maricopa County, Arizona who knew about the victims of these crimes it was Joe Arpaio.

I was outraged by the uncaring and callous manner in which Joe Arpaio referred to the many victims of these crimes – most of whom were children. Arpaio's public press conference prompted me to write a Letter to the Editor of the *Arizona Republic* newspaper in Phoenix. The letter was published by the newspaper both on-line at <u>www.azcentral.com</u> as well as in the printed newspaper. Here is the letter:

****

Sheriff Arpaio failed victims of El Mirage

By Bill Louis

I have first-hand knowledge of the incredible level of neglect on the part of Sheriff Joe Arpaio. I find it difficult to refrain from comment after seeing his "apology" to the victims of the dozens of serious sex crimes and child molestations that he failed to investigate in El Mirage.

His callous comment of *"if there were any victims"* shows his arrogance and the insincerity of his so-called apology. Arpaio knows full well there were many victims and he knows their identities. In 2008 the sheriff received a full written account of all the cases his office failed to investigate in El Mirage.

The Maricopa County Sheriff's Office had provided police services in El Mirage for three years. In mid-2007, the new leadership of the El Mirage Police Department took over.

A sheriff's deputy chief called El Mirage Police Chief Mike Frazier and told him to get the evidence from the El Mirage cases out of their property impound. The deputy chief also told Frazier he was returning all the police reports (several boxes) from the time period when the Sheriff's Office had been responsible for providing police services in El Mirage. That deputy chief told the El Mirage police administration that all the reports were "complete" and could just be "filed away." A few weeks later the boxes of police reports were returned to El Mirage.

At that time, I was the newly hired assistant police chief. For quality control purposes, I directed the El Mirage detectives to conduct a random sampling of the serious criminal cases (sex crimes and child molestations) that had been returned from Arpaio's office. (We were already in the process of reviewing several death investigations Arpaio's staff had mishandled.)

The cursory review showed that none of the sex crime and molesting cases had been completed. Most had not had any follow up done after the first-responder's contact.

I ordered a full review of the returned cases. To my dismay our full audit showed that none of the cases had been completed.

I notified my counterpart in Arpaio's office and told him of the apparent gross negligence we had found in the review of the cases he had returned to El Mirage. The deputy chief told me that we could return the cases to the Sheriff's Office and he would ensure that the cases would be re-opened and handled properly.

I told him, "Thanks, but no thanks." At that point, we had little confidence in Arpaio's ability to handle these serious criminal cases.

We informed the sheriff's staff that we would retain the cases and assign El Mirage detectives to re-investigate them. As law enforcement professionals we had an obligation to the victims of these serious crimes. It was now our responsibility to attempt to bring justice to the victims of these crimes that Arpaio's office had neglected.

We knew the task of re-investigating three years of neglected criminal cases would tax our limited El Mirage police resources. At our request, El Mirage City Manager B.J. Cornwall approved special funding and we temporarily hired some retired Phoenix detectives to re-investigate the neglected cases.

After months of extra work, the El Mirage Police Department staff finally completed the re-investigation of the neglected cases. A comprehensive report was completed including an overview and summary of each case. The report included information about every victim.

This report and a cover letter were sent to Sheriff Joe Arpaio. Although this was the professional and ethical manner to handle this situation, Arpaio had the audacity to criticize the El Mirage police department for preparing this report. He chastised us for "creating a public record" of his negligence. (This is the same Joe Arpaio who publicly questioned whether there really were any victims.)

Many months after we finished re-investigating the cases an Arizona Republic reporter uncovered this negligence by Arpaio and requested a public records request for the El Mirage Police report and the letter to the sheriff. When

Arpaio's negligence on these cases was made public in a subsequent news report, Arpaio announced he was launching an "internal investigation" into the matter.

That was nearly three years ago and Arpaio apparently still has not concluded his internal investigation. It seems that only when this issue is brought back onto the radar screen does Arpaio remember he was supposed to investigate it internally.

So, just how sincere was Sheriff Joe Arpaio in his apologetic comment about whether there are actual victims in the neglected El Mirage cases? He has known about it for at least three years. The facts of this situation speak for themselves.

Sheriff Joe Arpaio failed these victims. At this point there is little that can be done to undo the harm they have endured.

A sincere apology and acceptance of responsibility from Joe Arpaio to these victims would have been the professional and compassionate thing to do. But, instead we once again witnessed Arpaio's smug and defiant attitude — this time directed towards the very victims he neglected.

****

INTRODUCTION

By Bill Louis

Maricopa County Sheriff Joe Arpaio had provided police service to the city of El Mirage, Arizona for approximately 2½ years during 2005 to 2007. The city had a contract with the sheriff's office to provide police protection to its residents for approximately $2.5 million. Then in 2007 the city decided to re-organize its own police force. The contract with the Maricopa County Sheriff's Office was terminated and a "new" El Mirage Police Department was formed.

I was hired as the Assistant Police Chief of the newly formed El Mirage Police Department. After more than 30 years with the Phoenix Police I left one of the top level positions in the department and went to El Mirage to help re-build their police department.

Not long after we started in El Mirage our detective staff began reviewing the police reports from 2005-2007 when the Maricopa County Sheriff's Office had been in El

Mirage. The sheriff's office had returned boxes of reports to El Mirage and told us they were all "complete."

What we found during the review was unconscionable.

Dozens of cases involving homicides, robberies, and sex crimes had been mishandled, neglected or simply ignored by the Maricopa County Sheriff's Office. Most of the sex crimes involved small children. Some of the homicide cases had strong evidence and looked to be "solvable" but were just never completed.

In this book I provide the reader with a brief history of El Mirage, Arizona and its struggles with managing the growth that occurred during the housing boom. The city's population grew from 5,000 to 33,000 in just a few years. El Mirage's original police department was wrought with problems and mismanagement and was eventually disbanded.

As the El Mirage Assistant Police Chief from November 2007 until October 2010 I was responsible for the day-to-day operations of the police department. In addition, I was heavily involved in the department's Detective Unit which handled serious criminal investigations. This book includes many of my personal experiences as Assistant Police Chief in El Mirage.

The book also examines the city of El Mirage's relationship with the Maricopa County Sheriff's Office and the events which led to them signing a contract for police service in their city. The book also tells how El Mirage later became disenchanted with the Maricopa County Sheriff due to poor service, their lack of accountability and a general dissatisfaction by their residents.

But, most importantly, this book gives the reader an inside look at just how serious the level of neglect was in El Mirage by the Maricopa County Sheriff's Office. The types of crimes that were mishandled, what the victims endured and how the offenders were never brought to justice are all described in detail.

By reviewing the actual police reports, the book includes an in-depth account of 31 child sex-crime cases that were seriously mishandled by the Special Victims Unit of the Maricopa County Sheriff's Office in 2005-2007.

Each case includes a complete, real-life account of the crimes and how each was mishandled by the Maricopa County Sheriff's Office. The specific details about the crimes enumerated in this book are based on the actual police reports that were written by the first-responder police officers, deputies, detectives and supervisors.

The information in the police reports is from first-hand accounts of victims, witnesses, parents, social workers, teachers and friends who gave their statements to the police officers or deputies when the crimes were first reported to the Maricopa County Sheriff's Office.

Of course, the real names and addresses have all been changed to protect the victims, witnesses and suspects.

But, *If There Were Any Victims* is more than just an expose´ of poor police practices by Sheriff Joe Arpaio's organization. It also serves as an educational tool for parents and young people alike. Through the real life experiences of the victims and their families, parents can gain insight on ways to prevent their own children from becoming victims of child predators. Teachers can use the experiences of the victims in this book as topics of classroom discussion about running away from home, the dangers of the Internet and other high risk activities. Counselors can glean valuable insight from the circumstances which led the children in these incidents to become victimized.

The book is divided into three sections.

Section I provides background information about the El Mirage Police Department, the Maricopa County Sheriff's Office and the interaction between them.

Section I:

- A brief history of the city of El Mirage
- The disbanding of the El Mirage Police Department in 2005

- The contract with the Maricopa County Sheriff's Office for police service 2005-2007
- Why the contract with the sheriff's office suddenly stopped
- Building of a "new" El Mirage Police Department in 2007
- How the sheriff's office mishandled dozens of sex crimes cases in El Mirage.
- How the bungled cases were discovered by the new El Mirage police
- The relationship between the senior staff of the Maricopa County Sheriff's Office and the new El Mirage Police Department

Section II reviews the actual police reports of 31 child sex-crime cases that were mishandled by the Maricopa County Sheriff's Office. This section also provides information for parents, educators and young people about the dangers children face from child predators and other high risk activities.

Section II:

- Internet and Chat Room Dangers - plus 3 police reports
- Runaway Juveniles - plus 2 police reports
- Child Molesters and Pedophiles – plus 5 police reports
- "Live-in" boyfriends, step-fathers, house guests – plus 5 police reports

- Fathers who molest their biological children – plus 5 police reports
- Sexual assaults – plus 6 police reports
- Other sex crimes against children – plus 5 police reports

Section III of this book contains the final two chapters. Chapter 14 provides the reader with a summary of several other criminal investigations that were mishandled by the Maricopa County Sheriff's Office when they were providing police service in El Mirage. Specifically, these cases involve homicides, suicides and other death investigations.

The final chapter of the book is entitled *"Leadership and Lessons Learned."* This chapter analyzes the different qualities of effective leaders in law enforcement agencies.

In this chapter I reflect upon my personal experiences in dealing with the top levels of the Maricopa County Sheriff's Office from 2007 to 2010. I also state my opinions about the *lack* of real leadership by Sheriff Joe Arpaio.

Section III:

- Other Mishandled Investigations (death investigations)
- Leadership and Lessons Learned

A Shift in Priorities

For many years I had been a supporter of Sheriff Joe Arpaio - even when it wasn't popular to do so. Sheriff Arpaio was very popular among the people of Maricopa County getting himself re-elected to multiple 4-year terms. He was well-known for the "pink underwear" his jail inmates were required to wear and his "tent city" jail facility. He created a self-image that caused some people to believe he was "tough on crime."

But among other law enforcement professionals in the metro-Phoenix area Sheriff Arpaio was viewed in a different light. Local police chiefs generally viewed Joe Arpaio as ineffective in overall crime prevention, and more interested in grandstanding and self-promotion.

Over the years I saw a sharp decline in Sheriff Arpaio's effectiveness in running the Maricopa County Sheriff's Office. As professional lawmen many of us were disappointed to see Arpaio lose sight of his true responsibility – to provide effective police service to the residents of Maricopa County.

Instead, he all but turned his back on investigating serious local crimes and focused heavily on *"immigration enforcement."* As a result, many crime victims within his county were neglected and countless offenders escaped justice.

Illegal Immigration

The issue of illegal immigration has been a hot button topic in Arizona for many years. It has alienated our citizens and has caused lines to be drawn in the sand among the political parties. The Arizona state legislature passed useless and ineffective laws to try to combat illegal immigration that have no chance of working. The laws have brought negative and economic sanctions against our great state of Arizona.

As a career lawman, I am against illegal immigration as much as anyone. I recognize the social, economic and criminal problems that illegal immigrants cause in our country. I just don't believe that enforcing immigration laws should be the "primary focus" of any local law enforcement agency.

That job belongs in the hands of the federal government. And clearly the feds have failed Arizona and other border states in this area.

As a local cop I arrested countless illegal immigrants in my career. In each case I turned them over to the federal immigration authorities for disposition and deportation. But, in every one of those situations I already had the person in custody for a local criminal charge and subsequently determined they were in this country illegally.

In those cases I had come in contact with the person on a traffic stop, a domestic violence call, a bar fight or some other police activity and arrested them on a local charge.

Never did I do an "immigration sweep" looking for illegal immigrants in the city of Phoenix. To do so would have been counterproductive to the mission and goals of local law enforcement. It would have driven a wedge between the police and community. Besides, I was always too busy arresting real criminals and *properly* investigating crimes.

Urban law enforcement is a difficult and complex issue. A police department needs the trust of the community to be effective. They shouldn't fear law enforcement for the wrong reasons. If a person is victimized they should feel completely comfortable calling the police or sheriff department. They shouldn't worry about their "immigration status" if they have been the victim of a crime. If a community fears the police (or sheriff) and do not call when they are needed anarchy will soon prevail in that community.

Most local police agencies have an immigration enforcement policy. The policies of agencies such as the Phoenix Police Department and the El Mirage Police Department are fair and reasonable. They allow their officers the flexibility to arrest illegal immigrants, but also allow residents to know they can call the police when they need their help. This is a delicate balance. But, illegal immigration enforcement should *never* be a priority of any local police or sheriff department.

By 2006 I was no longer a supporter of Sheriff Joe Arpaio. To me his focus was nothing more than pandering to the popular "illegal immigration" issue in order to get re-elected.

His tactics became the focus of an FBI civil rights investigation and the United States Department of Justice deemed his practices to be unconstitutional.

In 2007 the new El Mirage Police Department discovered the mishandled criminal cases by the Maricopa County Sheriff's Office. The scandal was uncovered by investigative journalists several months later. The public soon became aware of the botched criminal investigations that occurred in El Mirage under Sheriff Joe Arpaio's watch.

Sheriff Arpaio received a flurry of negative national publicity when the mishandling of these cases was publicly exposed. On December 5, 2011 Sheriff Arpaio made a half-hearted apology to the victims of these crimes, but qualified his "apology" by questioning whether there *really were any victims*.

Perhaps this book will help Sheriff Joe Arpaio answer his own question of *"if there were any victims..."*

****

SECTION ONE

How It All Began

Chapters

CHAPTER 1

The Classless Farewell

The summer of 1976 in Phoenix was a particularly hot one. I had finished my military service in the U.S. Army including three years of overseas tours and was back home in Phoenix. By then I was married and already had one son. Our second child was on the way and due in December of that year. I was working for my parents as the manager of the Hermosa Inn.

I remember that particular day in August when I received my long-awaited notice from the City of Phoenix Personnel Department. "Congratulations," it read. "You have been selected for the position of POLICE OFFICER with the Phoenix Police Department." My lifelong passion of being a Phoenix Police officer was about to come true. I was assigned to Phoenix Police Academy Recruit Class 138.

Over the next nearly 31 years I lived my dream of being a Phoenix cop. I worked a variety of assignments and promoted through the ranks. My favorite assignment was always uniform patrol duty at every rank. I also got to work as an administrative sergeant in the Police Chief's Office. As a Police Lieutenant I was fortunate enough to get specialty assignments as the Basic Training Commander at the Academy, the Liaison to the City Manager, Employment Bureau Commander and Internal Affairs. As Police Commander I later led the Organized Crime Bureau, Professional Standards Bureau, the Downtown Bureau, the Violent Crimes Bureau and the Homeland Security Division as an Assistant Police Chief.

From my perspective I had been blessed with a complete and rewarding career having survived nearly 31 years as a cop.

The Farewell

But, it was now Friday, November 2, 2007. This was that elusive day that most career cops dream about.

My family was there as were friends, peers and colleagues from throughout the law enforcement community. Dozens of police chiefs and assistant chiefs, local heads of the ATF, FBI, Secret Service and U.S. Marshall's Office were in attendance. Prosecutors, defense attorneys, Phoenix City Council, citizens, city staffers and community leaders were seated in the audience and standing along the walls.

The special event room at the Burton Barr library in downtown Phoenix was jammed packed. I felt honored beyond words that so many colleagues and friends showed up to say "farewell" on my last day as Assistant Police Chief of the Phoenix Police Department.

The master-of-ceremonies was Phoenix Police Commander Jeff Halstead. Commander Halstead and I had worked together on the Phoenix Police Department. He and I were friends and I also had the ultimate respect for him as law enforcement professional. Jeff Halstead had a charismatic personality and a great sense of humor. He was the perfect host for a retirement gathering.

Everyone in the room was aware that the following Monday I would take the reins as Assistant Police Chief at the El Mirage Police Department. My former Phoenix Police colleague Mike Frazier was the new El Mirage Police Chief and he hired me as his Second in Command. My job would be to run the day-to-day operations of the police department in El Mirage.

Presentations

Phoenix Police Chief Jack Harris made one of the first presentations. He spoke about my tenure as an experienced investigator in the Phoenix Police Violent Crimes Bureau during the "Baseline Killer" and "Serial Shooter" cases. Chief Harris reminded the audience that I had headed up both of these serial murder investigations which resulted in the arrests and convictions of the killers in both cases.

(Beginning in the summer of 2005 the metro Phoenix area was being stalked by two separate but simultaneous "serial killers." The media dubbed them the "Serial Shooter" and "Baseline Killer." On August 2, 2006 Dale Hausner and Samuel Dieteman were arrested and charged with 8 murders and 19 attempted murders in connection with the "Serial Shooter" case. On September 6, 2006 Phoenix Police arrested Mark Goudeau in the "Baseline Killer" case and charged him with 8 murders and numerous other related felonies. Hausner, Dieteman and Goudeau were all subsequently convicted of the murders in the "Serial Shooter" and "Baseline Killer" cases. Here is a link to video clip by a local news station following the arrests of the Serial Shooters Hausner and Dieteman. http://www.youtube.com/watch?v=FnhxdSaJGPE)

At the conclusion of his presentation Chief Harris wished me luck in my future endeavors at the El Mirage Police Department and offered any assistance I might need from the Phoenix Police Department.

One of the next speakers was the Special Agent in Charge of the FBI Phoenix Office John Lewis. I had the pleasure of working with SAC Lewis for a few years particularly during my time as Chief of Homeland Security for the Phoenix Police Department. John Lewis epitomized what the FBI stood for in law enforcement professionalism. He always looked and acted like an FBI agent. Always courteous and never pompous, SAC Lewis always strived to maintain a great working relationship with local law enforcement officials. Mr. Lewis told the audience about our work together on some major investigations, the Joint Terrorism Task Force and security planning for the Super Bowl XLII in Phoenix. When SAC John Lewis concluded his comments, he presented me with a plaque on behalf of the FBI which read, *"In Recognition and Appreciation For Your Contributions to the Law Enforcement Community in the State of Arizona."* John concluded by publicly pledging the FBI's assistance in my new endeavors with the El Mirage Police Department.

The head of the federal Bureau of Alcohol, Tobacco and Firearms (BATF) Phoenix Field Division also made a presentation. Bill Newell was the Special Agent in Charge; he and I had worked together on a number of major investigations over the years. He talked about the effectiveness of our cooperative working relationship and my advocacy for the firearms forensic program known as NIBNS. As Bill Newell concluded his comments he said that if I ever need the assistance of the ATF in my new job in El Mirage to just give him a call. He then presented me with a beautiful bronze replica of the Arizona Lawman's memorial statue. The engraving said, *"In Appreciation For Your Dedicated Service To The City of Phoenix & to Valley Law Enforcement. Your Leadership & Friendship Shall Be Missed. Congratulations on Behalf of the ATF Phoenix Field Division."*

Special Agent in Charge Ken Huffer of the United States Secret Service also made a presentation. Ken commented about the many presidential visits we had worked together over the years as well as our working relationship on criminal investigations. He also offered the assistance of the Secret Service in my new position as the El Mirage Assistant Police Chief. Ken presented me with a plaque on behalf of the Secret Service that read, *"For Outstanding Assistance and Support on Behalf of the Investigative and Protective Responsibilities of the United States Secret Service."*

One by one the agency heads and others in attendance came to the podium and spoke of our shared law enforcement experiences. Some presented me with plaques and other mementos of appreciation. I was emotionally overwhelmed and humbled by the kindness of the comments made by my peers and colleagues. Each pledged to help me in any way in my new endeavors at the El Mirage Police Department.

The Maricopa County Sheriff's Office

Then came Chief Deputy Dave Hendershott representing the Maricopa County Sheriff's Office. I had known Hendershott professionally for many years. He was the "Second-in-Command" of the sheriff's office and reported directly to Sheriff Joe Arpaio.

I had many friends at the Maricopa County Sheriff's Office from line level deputies to members of the sheriff's "inner circle" executive staff. I had worked with members of the sheriff's office on countless occasions throughout my career. Together we worked criminal cases, trained together at the police academy and worked cooperatively on a variety of major investigations, task forces and special events like the 2001 World Series and the Super Bowl. Hendershott said a few words about my career and then read the words engraved on a plaque, *"In Appreciation For Your Many Years of Service to This Community, And The Cooperation You Have Offered So Many Agencies On That Effort. Good Luck And Good Fortune in Your Future Endeavors."* The plaque was signed, *"Joseph M. Arpaio, Maricopa County Sheriff."*

Hendershott handed me the plaque. As those in attendance applauded Hendershott leaned in close and said to me, *"El Mirage?? What the fuck are you thinking??"*

I looked at him and thought to myself that was such a "classless" thing to say to me at my farewell reception. At that very moment I knew that my working relationship with the Maricopa County Sheriff's Office was about to change forever.

What I *didn't* know was within a few weeks I would uncover a scandal about the Maricopa County Sheriff's Office during the time they provided police service in El Mirage, Arizona.

****

Chapter 2

How Law Enforcement Agencies Operate

Most mid-size and large American police and sheriff departments are organized and function in a similar manner. There are of course differences that make each organization unique, but the basic structure of American law enforcement agencies are pretty much the same throughout the country.

The history of American police agencies can be traced back to the police reforms in early nineteenth century England. Sir Robert Peel changed law enforcement forever when he drafted The Metropolitan Police Act of 1829 in London. This set of reforms established guidelines for law enforcement that are still in use today.

As suggested in Sir Robert Peel's reforms, most law enforcement agencies in the United States are organized and operate within a "paramilitary" format. That is, they wear uniforms, have rank structure and have a set of strict operational guidelines. Due to the nature of police work, regimentation and discipline are often deeply imbedded into the law enforcement culture.

The personnel who work in a police or sheriff's department are usually classified as either "sworn" or "civilian" employees.

The "sworn" employees are the police officers and deputies of all ranks. They have taken a special oath of office to uphold the law. The "civilian" or non-sworn employees are generally the professional support staff. Non-sworn employees fulfill important positions from entry-level file clerks to executive-level managers.

Within a police organization the "sworn" employees are typically addressed by their rank – Sergeant Smith, Captain Jones, etc.

By taking the law enforcement oath of office, "sworn" police officers and deputies are given a tremendous amount of authority, and are bound by law to follow the strict statutory and constitutional guidelines of their position. And with that authority comes tremendous responsibility.

Under the "color of authority" police officers have the lawful power to take away one of our most precious rights – our freedom *(stop, detain or arrest)*. And under certain circumstances police officers even have the authority to take a human life.

This level of power and authority is extended to no one other than law enforcement within the context of the United States Constitution.

The powers of the police in the United States should never be taken for granted. Individual officers and the leaders of police organizations should <u>always</u> be held accountable to the public for their actions.

Police chiefs and sheriffs have the responsibility to effectively supervise and manage the on-duty performance of the personnel within their organizations. They are directly accountable for the actions of the personnel within their agencies.

Police and sheriff departments typically consist of first-responders, detectives and support staff. Many large departments also have crime labs and/or crime scene specialists (such as in the TV show *CSI*) which handle the collection, preservation and analysis of crime scene evidence.

First Responders

The "first responders" are typically the uniformed officers and deputies you routinely see driving around in "marked" police cruisers. These are the officers who respond when you call 911 or the police for help. They drive fully marked police cars and are in full uniform so they are clearly recognized as the police when they arrive on the scene of an emergency.

The first responder officers are typically trained and equipped to handle most emergency situations as well as routine crime investigations such as thefts and traffic collisions. They are also trained to preserve evidence at major crime scenes for "specialty" personnel such as detectives or crime scene technicians to handle.

When a uniformed officer or deputy responds to a call and determines that it is a serious crime they typically notify a supervisor of the circumstances. The supervisor will routinely respond to the scene and assess whether more or specialty personnel are needed to handle the case. If so, the supervisor will normally request assistance.

Detectives

In most law enforcement agencies detectives are usually considered "specialty" officers. They typically have many years of experience in police work and have received advanced training in crime scene investigation, interview and interrogation techniques, and collection and preservation of evidence.

Many detectives develop an area of "expertise" (homicide, sex crimes, etc.) and receive technical and forensic training in their particular area.

Specialty training among detectives can include:

> "Blood spatter" from gunshot wounds
> Collecting DNA and other "trace evidence" from victims/crime scenes
> "Forensic interviewing" child sex-crime victims
> Crime scene reconstruction
> Preparing and executing search warrants

Detectives will typically be called to handle violent crimes, serious assaults (shootings, stabbings, etc.), sex crimes and homicides. Property crimes with significant losses or unusual circumstances may also be assigned to detectives.

Once a detective has been assigned or notified of a case they become the "case agent" for the investigation. They are then responsible for any and all follow-up investigation and to bring the case to a conclusion. When they complete the investigation the detective is responsible to submit the case to the prosecuting agency to bring charges against the suspect.

But, detectives don't always have to respond to the scene of a serious crime. This is typically the case when a crime is reported after-the-fact and there is no urgency for a detective at the crime scene.

For example, a 6 year-old girl reports that her mother's former live-in boyfriend had molested her in the past. The ex-boyfriend has moved out so the child is no longer in any immediate danger. The officer would notify a supervisor who would then call a specialty detective.

In this case there would be no need for the detective to immediately respond to the scene. The detective would likely ask the on-scene officer to complete his report and send it to him/her with all the pertinent information (contact information for the victim, mother, ex-boyfriend, etc.). The "follow-up" investigation on the case could be handled by the detective later that day or the next day.

The term "follow-up" is used in a broad sense as it pertains to detectives. Follow-up by detectives can include a host of activities and investigative strategies. Depending on the type of crime, those activities might include: an in-depth interview of the victim; interviews with witnesses, relatives and neighbors; a search warrant to collect evidence; identifying and locating the suspect; and arresting and interrogating the suspect.

Support Staff

Probably the most underrated yet equally important members of any law enforcement agency are their professional support staff. The employees who work in these administrative positions are normally "civilian" (not police officers) members of the organization. They often work behind the scenes in the less "glamorous" positions on the police department.

These critical staff personnel answer the phones and 911 emergency lines; input, track and analyze crime data and statistics; dispatch the officers to calls for service; manage enormous police records systems; store and track massive quantities of police evidence in warehouses; and, they ensure that the I/T and high-tech police communications systems work properly.

The head of any police agency in the country will tell you their department could not function without the dedicated members of their support staff.

Law Enforcement in Arizona

There are over 15,000 local, county, and state law enforcement officers in Arizona. The majority of those "sworn" officers work for city or town police departments, the Arizona Department of Public Safety (state police), sheriff's offices or state university campus police departments.

_A.Z.P.O.S.T._

In Arizona "sworn" police officers and deputies of all ranks are regulated by a state board known as the Arizona Peace Officers Standards and Training board

(A.Z.P.O.S.T.). They establish hiring, training and retention standards for all city, state and county law enforcement officers in Arizona.

The A.Z.P.O.S.T. board determines the minimum standard requirements to be hired by a law enforcement agency in Arizona. The board requires a hiring agency to perform a full background investigation and drug screen of all police applicants. If the applicant meets all the hiring requirements they are allowed to enter a police academy approved by the A.Z.P.O.S.T. board.

Upon successful completion of the rigorous police academy training program the applicants are "certified" as Arizona peace officers by A.Z.P.O.S.T. and may begin working at a police or sheriff department. Once they have been "certified" the applicants take their law enforcement Oath of Office and become "sworn" police officers or deputies.

The A.Z.P.O.S.T. board also has the authority to revoke or suspend a police officer's certification for cause. The board establishes standards for serious misconduct and can "de-certify" police officers prohibiting them from working in a peace officer capacity in Arizona. Officers accused of serious misconduct are entitled to "due process" through A.Z.P.O.S.T. and are afforded a hearing before the board.

(Federal officers, correctional or detention officers are not regulated by AZPOST.)

County Sheriffs in Arizona

The state of Arizona is divided into 15 counties. Each county has an elected sheriff who holds the office for a four-year term.

Per the Arizona Constitution each county sheriff runs a county jail for their jurisdiction. Adults convicted of misdemeanor crimes serve their sentences in the county jails. Arrestees awaiting trial on misdemeanor and felony crimes, as well as fugitives awaiting extradition and people awaiting deportation are also housed in the county jails.

The Arizona Constitution also requires that each county sheriff provides full law enforcement services to all "unincorporated areas" of their respective county. That generally means any area within the county except incorporated cities and towns that provide their own police service.

Maricopa County is located in the central part of the state of Arizona. It is named after a proud, indigenous Native American group from the region.

Maricopa County includes the metro-Phoenix area and has a population of over 4,000,000 people. Other large cities including Mesa, Glendale, Peoria, Scottsdale, Tempe, Chandler, Gilbert and Surprise are all located within Maricopa County.

Any local town or city in Arizona may also negotiate a contract with their local county to have the sheriff provide full or supplemental law enforcement service within their town or city for an annual fee. This is usually done by smaller towns and cities who cannot afford their own police department.

Such was the case with the city of El Mirage, Arizona.

From October 2005 until October 2007 Maricopa County Sheriff Joe Arpaio's office was paid to provide full law enforcement services to the residents of El Mirage.

Much of the information in this book relates to the actions and performance of the Maricopa County Sheriff's Office while they provided police service to the residents of El Mirage, Arizona.

****

CHAPTER 3

El Mirage, Arizona

A suburb just west of Phoenix, El Mirage is a small city with a present-day population of about 33,000. It might be considered a bedroom community with very few businesses and no industry. The major source of sales tax revenue is a large Wal-Mart store on the city's west side. There is one gas station, one fast food restaurant and the city has no banks. The older section of town is dotted with Mexican restaurants, mini-marts and auto repair shops.

The City of El Mirage has more than 130 employees in various departments and has an annual operating budget of roughly $80 million. El Mirage has the typical council-manager form of government. The city manager runs the day-to-day operations of the city, and the Mayor/City Council create policy and budgets.

The city was incorporated in 1951 and the population remained around 5,000 for decades. When the housing boom hit in 2002-03, the city expanded to 11 square miles and the population exploded to nearly 40,000. The 2008 recession and housing slump took their toll on many El Mirage residents and foreclosures were rampant. The 2010 U.S. census put the population of El Mirage at 33,000.

The city was originally settled on a one square mile plot and was home to mostly migrant workers. A proud and strong Hispanic influence is still very evident in sections of present day El Mirage.

A Community Under Strain

For many years El Mirage had a reputation as a troubled community. A series of scandalous incidents and corruption in the small city government gave them a black eye that never seemed to go away. But, when the city began to grow the residents knew it was time to change their image and make reforms.

In October of 2004 the City of El Mirage partnered with Arizona State University to hold a series of community forums. Participants included El Mirage residents and business owners, city staff, community and religious leaders and local educators. The process was facilitated by professionals from ASU West. The purpose was to get a grass roots opinion of what was good and bad about living in El Mirage – directly from the residents. The program was entitled ***An Assessment of Community Needs, Assets and Vision Within El Mirage.***

The residents described living in El Mirage as *"A Community Under Strain."* The population had quadrupled in the previous 4 years and the per capita police staffing levels dropped 50%, while police calls increased five-fold. The juvenile drug arrest rate was 5 times the county average and the adult drunken driving arrest rate was 420 times the county average. The birthrate among juveniles was 4 times the national average. The last census indicated that 16% of the population of El Mirage was living in poverty. The per capita food stamp rate was 3 times higher than the county average. A concurrent study showed that the city of El Mirage had sub-par performance on 23 of 25 indicators that comprise the Arizona Department of Health Services' "Community Risk Profile."

A Vision for the Future

But, a number of positives also came out of the forum. These were listed by the group as *"COMMUNITY ASSETS."*

The residents of El Mirage were proud of their rich family ties with many generations still living in the community. The group cited affordable housing and a great opportunity for growth as positive reasons for living in El Mirage.

At the end of the forum the participants developed a vision for the future of El Mirage. They described it as *"A VISION FOR THE FUTURE – 7 PILLARS."* The seven pillars of vision for the future included:

1. Strong Community Recreation and Education Programs

2. Community Revitalization

3. Sufficient Infrastructure for Growth

4. Dependable Public Transportation

5. Expanded Human Services

6. Safe Streets and Safe Community

7. Vibrant Citizen Involvement

It was clear that the El Mirage city leaders and residents really cared about their community and were serious about improving the quality of life. They had quantified their concerns and everyone knew that something had to be done. It was now up to the city manager and Mayor/City Council to take the appropriate steps to get it started.

A Police Department In Need Of Reform

Until the year 2005 the city of El Mirage had its own police department. The police chief was formerly under the supervision of the mayor and *not* the city manager - which led to a myriad of problems. In the 1970's and early 1980's there were even allegations of corruption within the police department; but those bad apples were eventually weeded out.

By 2004 the city was in the midst of a tremendous population growth. An infusion of property tax revenues was breathing new life into the small town. A new air of professionalism was on the horizon for the city government of El Mirage. The El Mirage city council hired a forward-thinking city manager and moved the police department under him.

By that time, the El Mirage police department was made up of mostly hard-working and dedicated police officers. The officers themselves realized that years of ineffective leadership had tarnished their reputation. They rallied together and went to the city manager asking for help. The veteran officers of the beleaguered El Mirage Police Department hoped that reform was finally on the way.

Wanting to determine the true scope of the problem, El Mirage City Manager B.J. Cornwall commissioned a professional consulting firm in 2005 to conduct a thorough audit of the El Mirage Police Department. The audit examined the previous five fiscal years of the police department's operations.

The findings of the study were staggering. The consulting firm uncovered a lack of accountability at the higher levels of the police department. The report showed a history of poor police practices, neglected cases and widespread mismanagement. They found evidence from crime scenes was routinely mishandled or misplaced; a haphazard patrolling system; poor case management and low clearance rates; and, an overall lack of accountability. They found deficiencies in every aspect of police service.

The consultant's final report described the El Mirage Police Department as the "most dysfunctional police department" it had ever seen.

The Sheriff Comes to Town

The consultant's final report proved what the El Mirage city manager already knew – the El Mirage Police Department was broken. The manager had to do something to restore order and credibility to the growing city. So, in 2005 he negotiated a contract with the Maricopa County Sheriff's Office to provide police service for the residents of El Mirage.

The sheriff's office brought in their own uniformed deputies, supervisors and command staff. A dozen or so veteran El Mirage police officers remained to work under the supervision of the sheriff's command. Those officers and the uniformed sheriff deputies patrolled the streets of El Mirage.

The city's contract with the Maricopa County Sheriff's Office meant that the sheriff was responsible for all aspects of police service and law enforcement activities.

From routine patrol to major investigations, Sheriff Joe Arpaio and his staff were now fully responsible to protect the residents of El Mirage. That meant respond to 911 calls, investigate crimes, arrest offenders, collect evidence, supervise employees, and manage criminal cases. In the most serious of crimes, the Sheriff's Homicide Unit or Special Victims Unit would be called in to investigate.

In the typical fashion of Maricopa County Sheriff Joe Arpaio, the logos from the sheriff's office were implanted everywhere in El Mirage – on police cars, the command van, buildings and stationary. There was no doubt to the residents of El Mirage that Sheriff Joe Arpaio was now in charge of law enforcement in their city.

The sheriff employees began to correct a number of the deficiencies that had existed at the El Mirage Police Department. They gathered up all the evidence from crimes and transported it to their evidence warehouse. They implemented some new operational policies and patrol procedures. Their Internal Affairs unit initiated some long overdue investigations of misconduct by a few El Mirage employees. It appeared, at least on the surface, that police service in El Mirage was starting to improve.

Dissatisfaction With The Sheriff

But, the progress with the Maricopa County Sheriff's Office was short-lived. Over the next two years more and more residents of El Mirage became disenchanted with the level of service they were receiving from the Maricopa County Sheriff's Office.

The El Mirage city manager, mayor and city council received numerous complaints about dispatch issues — long waits, dropped calls, slow response times, and a decrease in Spanish-language services for non-emergency calls. The residents complained at open forums about their lack of feeling safe in their homes and never seeing a police car in their neighborhood.

Even the dozen or so El Mirage Police officers who remained working under the umbrella of the Maricopa County Sheriff's Office were lodging complaints to the city manager. They felt there was a clear disparity with the way they were treated by the sheriff's supervisors compared to the deputies.

The officers also voiced their concerns to the sheriff's command staff about the lack of supervision and accountability of the deputies assigned to patrol duties in

El Mirage. The officers said the sheriff's deputies were constantly "sitting around the (police) station" while the El Mirage officers were on the streets patrolling and answering 911 calls for service.

And, whenever "less desirable" calls for service were dispatched it was always an El Mirage officer who handled the calls. The El Mirage officers said the Maricopa County Sheriff's deputies were "nowhere to be found."

When these veteran El Mirage officers tried to bring these issues to the attention of Maricopa County Sheriff's supervisors their concerns were dismissed as "petty" or simply ignored.

Contract With Sheriff Arpaio Terminated

As the complaints about poor service from the residents of El Mirage mounted, the El Mirage city manager decided it was time to re-build the El Mirage Police Department. In August 2007 he notified the Maricopa County Sheriff's Office he was terminating the contract with them for police service in El Mirage. That didn't set well with Sheriff Joe Arpaio.

The contract with the Maricopa County Sheriff's Office officially ended on October 13, 2007 and Sheriff Joe Arpaio wasn't about to go out quietly. Instead of bidding farewell and thanking the residents of El Mirage in a graceful and professional manner, Sheriff Joe Arpaio made his exit in his usual grandstanding manner.

On the last night of providing police service to the residents of El Mirage he brought in his entourage and did one of his infamous "immigration sweeps." Complete with his posse and armored vehicles he caravanned through the small city for all to see. And of course no "Sheriff Joe" event would be complete without his press conference and TV cameras. And so ended the two-year reign of Sheriff Joe Arpaio in El Mirage.

It was no secret that Sheriff Arpaio was irate when he lost the contract and millions of dollars in revenue from the city of El Mirage. According to those close to him he believed all along that a contract renewal with El Mirage was a near certainty.

And Sheriff Arpaio was even less-happy to find out the El Mirage city manager was hiring some Phoenix Police veterans to take over the police department.

****

CHAPTER 4

The New El Mirage Police Department

The plan was to hire a new police chief and command staff for the El Mirage Police Department. The city manager's goal was to completely revamp the police department with all new leadership, new employees, new policies and a fresh new image of professionalism.

The search for a new police chief didn't last too long. A veteran police executive was retiring from the Phoenix Police Department and was interested in the position. In early September 2007 the City of El Mirage announced that former Phoenix Executive Assistant Police Chief Michael T. Frazier would be the new Police Chief of El Mirage. On October 8, 2007 Frazier took the helm at the El Mirage Police Department.

A month later on November 5, 2007 I was hired as Frazier's Second-in-Command (Assistant Police Chief) and the work was about to begin.

The El Mirage Police Station

The city of El Mirage is a Phoenix suburb located in the far northwest part of the Valley of the Sun (metro-Phoenix area). Although I lived in the Phoenix area most of my life, I had only passed through El Mirage on a few occasions. I remembered it only as a tiny 'blip on the radar screen' when driving to Las Vegas.

I had been to the El Mirage Police station only once during my career with the Phoenix Police Department. I hardly even remember it now. It was probably around 1979 or 1980 when I was working in a plainclothes assignment. We had been tracking down an armed robbery suspect and the trail led us to El Mirage.

As I look back on it today, I remember the police station in El Mirage as small and old-looking. It was located in an area of the town that made me glad I was carrying a gun.

My partner and I met with an El Mirage officer to assist us in their city. The one thing that I specifically remember was the El Mirage officer's uniform looked terrible. His uniform pants and shirt didn't match; his gunbelt consisted of mismatched items; his uniform shoes were scuffed and he needed a haircut.

I remember how good it felt to get back to the Phoenix Police Department that day.

Day One

It was November 5, 2007 and I was driving to El Mirage for my first day as the new Assistant Police Chief. All I could think about was the poor reputation of the "old" El Mirage Police Department. For years some Phoenix Police officers believed the El Mirage Police Department was corrupt and unprofessional. And now I was going to work there.

When I arrived that morning the police station wasn't exactly as I remembered it from 27 years earlier. The administrative offices of the El Mirage Police Department were in a modular building that resembled a double-wide trailer or a temporary school building.

I went inside and was greeted by the police department support staff in the visitor's lobby. They seemed very nice and truly made me feel welcome.

I was shown the way to my new office and saw my new boss Police Chief Mike Frazier along the way. We talked for a few minutes and before I had a chance to put my briefcase down it seemed like Frazier had already given me *five projects!*

Chief Frazier showed me to my new office and left me to unpack my things. I was immediately hit with a "reality check."

My office at El Mirage was is in the "double-wide" and measured about 10'x12'. I looked around in shock and yelled out to Frazier, *"There are no <u>windows</u> in here!"*

Three days earlier I had been an Assistant Police Chief with the Phoenix Police Department. I had a spacious office located on the top floor of the Phoenix Police headquarters building in downtown Phoenix. One entire wall of my office was windows overlooking the Phoenix skyline.

Now I was the Assistant Police Chief at the El Mirage Police Department and working in a tiny office with no windows.

My New Boss

Mike Frazier was no stranger to me. I had known Mike for nearly 30 years and we had worked together on many occasions at the Phoenix Police Department. We had a mutual respect for each other although our leadership styles were inherently different.

Chief Frazier has always been a man of the highest integrity and a consummate professional. But, his brain always ran at "mach speed" and he was a true workaholic in every sense of the word. (On countless mornings I would find work-related e-mails that Mike had written at 2:00 or 3:00 a.m. *Apparently the man never slept!*)

After I unpacked Chief Frazier showed me around the rest of the "modular" administration building. Not far from my office were the cramped quarters of the Detective Unit. The area was a hodge-podge of old, non-matching office furniture. There were two detectives working in the area. One of them was a former Phoenix Police detective hired by Chief Frazier two weeks earlier. The other was an El Mirage detective who had been there for several years. Chief Frazier *"mentioned"* that I needed to hire 3 more detectives and a Detective Sergeant.

The rest of the administration building included small offices for the secretarial staff and Police Records. At the far end of the building were the offices of the Administrative Sergeant, Community Action Officer and the department's Training Officer. Chief Frazier *"mentioned"* that I needed to recruit and hire a Crime Analyst and locate some office space in the administration building for the analyst.

The chief then showed me around the rest of the El Mirage Police Department compound. A new property/evidence warehouse had just been erected in the middle of the complex. It was also a modular building sitting on concrete pillars. Eventually, the storage building would house all the El Mirage Police crime scene evidence that was still at the Maricopa County Sheriff's Office evidence warehouse. The chief *"mentioned"* that he wanted me to recruit and hire a new Property Custodian to manage the warehouse.

This was the first hour of my first day. But, Chief Frazier didn't hesitate to *"mention"* that I also needed to "figure out a plan" to transfer the evidence from the sheriff's facility to ours. I would soon find out the nature of his urgency for this plan.

As we walked across the rest of the police compound Chief Frazier also *"mentioned"* that he wanted me to recruit and hire a Crime Scene Specialist to help the detectives at crime scenes.

The chief and I then walked into the "Patrol Building." This was the old, original brick building I remembered as the El Mirage Police station from my one visit to El Mirage many years earlier.

The building had one long corridor with a low ceiling and a few offices on both sides. It had a small briefing room and a work area with computer work stations for the officers to type their reports. The restrooms and a small break room were in the middle of the building and two prisoner cells were at the far end. And, of course, Chief Frazier *"mentioned"* that I needed to recruit and hire about 15 more police officers.

I had now toured the entire El Mirage Police facility - the modular administration building, the evidence warehouse and the old Patrol building. When I walked through the parking lots I noticed that the compound was not enclosed by a fence or wall. I recognized this as a serious security issue for our officers and staff. I was sure I'd be "tasked" with getting a security fence around the police department compound.

By the end of my first day I realized things were going to be different than what I had expected as the Assistant Police Chief of the El Mirage Police Department.

Goals of the "New" El Mirage Police Department

But, as different as the environment was in El Mirage I soon became completely entrenched in the job. I was truly excited about the prospect of creating a professional reputation for the El Mirage Police Department.

It didn't take long for me develop a deep fondness for this smaller police department and the city of El Mirage. I proudly wore my El Mirage Police uniform to work every day.

Our sights were set and the expectations were high. We were to re-build and re-engineer a police department that was once described as "dysfunctional."

The city council approved a new pay scale for Police Department employees which elevated the pay for El Mirage Police officers to the highest in the state of Arizona. With the higher pay scale we would be able to attract the best police officers. The council also approved a hefty "hiring bonus" to help us lure experienced, veteran police officers from other police departments.

The city council also approved the hiring of several specialty support staff personnel to allow us to build a complete, professional police department. All told, we were to hire 30 new people to fill the positions in the "new" El Mirage Police Department.

Former El Mirage Officers and Staff Personnel

A number of El Mirage police officers, supervisors and support staff remained from the previous administration and had survived the sheriff's time in El Mirage. They had a great deal of first-hand experience and historical perspective about El Mirage.

Except for a few, these tenured men and women from the former El Mirage Police Department were good employees. Most were dedicated and hard-working individuals who really cared about their police department. It took only a few days for me to realize that the troubles which had plagued the "old" El Mirage Police Department were not a result of bad employees - the problem was a lack of real leadership.

New El Mirage Officers and Support Personnel

In addition to the employees who remained in El Mirage, we set out to expand the capabilities of the police department by adding more officers, detectives, a Crime Analyst, a Crime Scene Technician and a Property Custodian to oversee evidence.

Over 30 new El Mirage Police employees would be hired during the coming months. This was no small task given the rigid hiring standards and background investigation requirements for police officers in Arizona.

We established a Detective Unit with a Detective Sergeant, 5 detectives and an Investigative Assistant. Patrol Operations was beefed up with new police officers and supervisors. A Crime Analyst was hired to provide "real-time" crime statistics to the patrol officers, detectives and residents of El Mirage.

The modular structure had been erected to warehouse police property and evidence. We hired a professional Property/Evidence Custodian to oversee and properly manage the impounded evidence. And finally, a Crime Scene Technician was hired and a fully out-fitted Crime Scene Response van was purchased. A new records management system was implemented for completing, storing and retrieving police reports.

A fleet of new black and white marked police cars was purchased along with 3 new police motorcycles. And, each police patrol car was now equipped with a high-tech Mobile Data Computer terminal. The Police

Communication Dispatchers assigned calls for service to the officers through the use of their mobile computers. The officers could now run instant warrant checks on individuals they stopped, check the status of driver and vehicle licenses, and type their police reports – all from their police cars.

And yes, a new perimeter security fence was installed around the police compound.

In a matter of six months the "new" El Mirage Police Department had become fully staffed. The shiny new "black and white" patrol cars were on the streets of El Mirage. The new officers, supervisors and support staff had all been hired and the Patrol Division was fully staffed. A Detective Sergeant, new detectives, an Investigative Assistant and a Crime Scene Specialist were now handling all the major crime scenes. A Crime Analyst was on board and using the latest high-tech software to track crime in El Mirage. A Property Custodian was running the evidence warehouse and had nearly completed the transfer of El Mirage's old evidence from the Sheriff's warehouse.

The men and women of the "new" El Mirage Police Department were now proudly serving the residents of El Mirage as a fully functioning, professional police department.

And, all of these accomplishments were made by the El Mirage Police Department despite the *lack of cooperation* afforded them by the Maricopa County Sheriff's Office.

****

CHAPTER 5

Political Enemies

Anyone who has lived in Arizona for a while knows about Sheriff Joe Arpaio and what he has done to those who have crossed him. He routinely labeled people with an opposing opinion to him as his "political enemies." The sheriff often targeted those people with "criminal investigations" and stopped at nothing to make their lives' miserable.

Sheriff Arpaio has gone after judges, county supervisors, newspaper editors and even the county's superintendent of schools. All because they voiced an opinion contrary to his own. He seemed to stop at nothing to hurt people, destroy their careers and publicly embarrass them.

And the most distressing fact was the vast majority of the charges he brought against people were inflated, baseless and were eventually tossed out of court. But, that didn't stop Joe Arpaio. Most of those individuals spent months or even years trying to defend themselves against the trumped up charges.

Many spent thousands of dollars in defense costs. In the end the charges were usually dropped but not before the people's lives had been turned upside down by the harassment from the Maricopa County Sheriff's Office.

Personally Victimized

I have spent nearly all of my adult life serving my country and community - as a soldier and a police officer. I dedicated my life to defending and protecting the rights of Americans.

And yet I became a victim of Sheriff Joe Arpaio's harassment after I voted against him in the 2008 election. As an American I always believed my right to vote would be protected. Not quite.

It was early Spring in 2008 and I had been employed at the El Mirage Police Department for just a few months. One day my boss returned from a meeting and asked to see me in his office.

Chief Frazier told me he just got back from a meeting with El Mirage Mayor Fred Waterman. The mayor related to Chief Frazier that he had recently been at an event where Sheriff Arpaio was present. The mayor said that the sheriff approached him and mentioned my name.

Mayor Waterman said that Arpaio told him that he "didn't like" me and that I was his "political enemy." When the mayor asked him why, Arpaio informed him that I had made a "campaign contribution" to his opponent. Apparently, Sheriff Arpaio felt that Mayor Waterman "needed to know" this information about my *personal* voting record. The mayor said that Arpaio was apparently trying to discredit me in the mayor's eyes.

It was clear that Arpaio felt that telling the mayor this information would somehow jeopardize my career at the El Mirage Police Department. But, unbeknownst to Joe Arpaio, Mayor Waterman was not a "Sheriff Joe" fan either. The mayor said he supported me and that my job in El Mirage would never be in jeopardy over who I voted for.

Nonetheless, hearing this really upset me. I always believed my voting rights were personal and constitutionally protected - one of the freedoms I fought to defend.

But, Sheriff Joe Arpaio doesn't seem to care about that – he likes to dig into people's personal lives. Campaign contribution records are considered "public records" so

Arpaio routinely digs up those records and uses them any way he wants.

The fact is I *did* make a contribution to his opponent - the "Dan Saban for Sheriff" campaign. Dan was a law enforcement colleague I had known for 25 years. I trusted and respected Dan Saban and felt he would make a good sheriff in Maricopa County.

I later found out that Joe Arpaio's staff routinely obtains the campaign contribution records of his opponents and scans them to find names he can target with harassment. And the new Assistant Police Chief in El Mirage must have looked like a good target. Lucky for me his harassment strategy didn't work this time.

This whole matter deeply disturbed me and still does today. I had served my country honorably and had a stellar police career. But, after 34+ years of defending my country and community I was apparently now walking around with a target on my back as an "enemy" of the county sheriff.

And all of this simply because I supported a different candidate. When all this occurred I told Chief Frazier it felt as if I was living in 1939 Nazi Germany.

Uncooperative and Unprofessional

Very soon after taking over the "new" El Mirage Police Department we realized Sheriff Joe Arpaio and his staff were not going to cooperate with us. It was very clear that this direction was coming directly from the top of the Maricopa County Sheriff's Office.

After first arriving in El Mirage in early November 2007 I spent the better part of two weeks sorting though the myriad of paperwork left behind by the Maricopa County Sheriff's Office staff. Most of it was self-explanatory and I figured out on my own what it was.

But there were dozens of other unexplained papers and documents involving on-going internal investigations, undercover funds, purchases, etc. I was at a loss as to the status of these items without input from the sheriff's staff who had initiated them.

I placed several phone calls to the sheriff's office trying to get the answers I needed. These phone calls soon became an exercise in futility.

When someone actually answered the phone, I identified myself and was immediately put on "hold." When someone finally came back on the line I was always told the person I was calling for was "unavailable." I left messages but no one ever called me back. It didn't take long to figure out that these Maricopa County Sheriff's Office commanders were either unprofessional or just playing games with me.

As the items began to pile up on my desk I gave some of them to my staff to resolve. Perhaps a sergeant would have better luck calling a peer at the sheriff's office. It certainly wasn't working at my level.

Eventually, I simply made decisions on dealing with the items that we couldn't get resolved through the sheriff's office. Some resulted in new investigations or required people to be re-interviewed. This created a lot of extra work, but at least we got it done – no thanks to the Maricopa County Sheriff's Office.

Interesting Finds

During the first week in El Mirage I was settling in to my office (which was previously occupied by the Maricopa County Sheriff's staff). I found a number of interesting and unexplainable items in the desk and file cabinets. In the back of a drawer in my desk I found a Glock 9mm pistol. In the back of a file cabinet I found an envelope containing cash with the words "U.C. funds" scribbled on the envelope.

I made several attempts to determine the origin of these items by calling the commanders at the Maricopa County Sheriff's Office but they never returned my calls. I finally just impounded these items into the El Mirage Police Department evidence lockers.

Property Room Evidence

Those first days and weeks in El Mirage were long and difficult. The transition from the Maricopa County

Sheriff's Office to a "new" El Mirage Police Department would be challenging.

It felt like not a day went by that we didn't receive some backlash from Sheriff Joe Arpaio's office.

Within the first week of Police Chief Frazier's new job in El Mirage he was contacted by a top commander in Arpaio's office. The Sheriff's commander told Chief Frazier to arrange to have all the crime scene evidence from El Mirage cases removed from the sheriff's property warehouse - immediately. *All the evidence!*

This was an impossible task and an unreasonable demand by the Maricopa County Sheriff's Office. Thousands of items had to be transferred. Chief Frazier had just taken over the police department and was not yet prepared for such a request. He had just obtained a portable warehouse for the El Mirage Police Department but had not yet hired a Property Custodian to transfer the evidence.

Crime Scene Evidence 101

Every police officer understands the importance of properly handling crime scene evidence. For those who are not familiar with the process of handling evidence here is some background information that may help explain why it is so important.

When a police officer or detective investigates a crime they generally collect evidence from the crime scene. Evidence can be as common as latent fingerprints collected and taped onto a card, or audio recordings of victim, witness or suspect interviews on a cassette tape or a CD. Photographs are taken at nearly every crime scene and impounded as evidence by police officers.

Evidence from serious crimes includes guns, knives, bullet casings, ropes and countless other things that may have been used in the commission of a violent crime. Biological evidence such as DNA, blood and semen are extremely important items of forensic evidence and have to be preserved through special processes.

Recovered stolen property that needs to be returned to its lawful owner is the most common item stored by the police in a property impound warehouse.

Just as important as the evidence itself is the manner in which the police handle the evidence. The "chain of custody" is an important legal term that deals with evidence of a crime and who handled it. This strict accountability process is critical to maintain the integrity of the evidence.

From the moment an item of evidence is seized by the police at a crime scene until it is presented in court, prosecutors have to account for every person who handled that piece of evidence.

An unexplained "break" in the "chain of custody" could be grounds for an item of evidence to be tossed out of court *and allow a suspect to go free. Rightfully so, defense attorneys often challenge the "chain of custody" of evidence by questioning everyone who handled the evidence.*

The Transfer

Everyone was aware that transferring thousands of items of evidence from the sheriff's warehouse to El Mirage would be a daunting task. Each piece would have to be handled in a manner that would not jeopardize the criminal cases associated with the evidence.

In order to maintain the "chain of custody" for court, each packaged item of evidence would have to be opened, identified and inventoried, and then re-packaged, transported and re-impounded into the El Mirage Police evidence room. A report would have to be written documenting each item that was handled and who handled it. There were thousands of items of evidence to be processed and the task could easily take months to complete.

But, the Maricopa County Sheriff's Office didn't seem to care. They informed the El Mirage Police Department that Sheriff Arpaio wanted the evidence out of _his_ warehouse and he wanted it out *"now."*

As unbelievable as it sounds, word came down to us from the Maricopa County Sheriff's Office that if El Mirage didn't remove the evidence Arpaio's warehouse "right away" the sheriff's office was going to "dump it off in our driveway." We knew this was a threat Sheriff Arpaio wouldn't carry out. To do so would jeopardize too many criminal cases. That would create "negative press" for the sheriff who thrives on publicity.

We eventually found a commander in the Maricopa County Sheriff's Office who was reasonable and willing to work with us to get the job accomplished properly. He was the brother of a Maricopa County Sheriff sergeant I had known for many years.

In November 2007 we hired a Property Custodian and a retired Phoenix Police detective to work full time transferring the evidence from the sheriff's warehouse to El Mirage's new evidence warehouse. The task eventually took six months to complete.

Booking Prisoners into Jail

Maricopa County is one of the largest counties in the United States. It has over 9,000 square miles and includes the entire metropolitan Phoenix area.

With only a few exceptions, the Maricopa County Sheriff's Office has the constitutional responsibility to house Maricopa County arrestees and anyone serving time for the conviction of a misdemeanor.

Local police departments are required to book their prisoners into the sheriff's jail. A few cities in Arizona operate their own jails and can house their own misdemeanor prisoners. Otherwise, all new arrestees (misdemeanors and felonies) have to be driven to the "main jail" on 4th Ave. & Madison Street in downtown Phoenix for booking.

For cities like El Mirage the distance to the sheriff's downtown Phoenix jail is 44 miles round trip. The average time for an El Mirage officer to transport a prisoner to the jail, complete the booking process and return to their beat area averages about 2 hours. During rush hour and on busy weekend nights the entire booking process can easily take up to 3 hours.

For many years the Maricopa County Sheriff's Office operated a satellite jail facility in the city of Surprise. The temporary jail served as a drop off point for arrestees for the nearby police departments of El Mirage, Surprise, Peoria, Youngtown and Wickenburg.

The facility accepted arrestees during peak periods of the day from about 10:00 am to 10:00 pm. The sheriff's detention crew would load up the prisoners into a jail transport van and drive the arrestees to the main jail in downtown Phoenix and book them.

This service saved the police officers from the nearby cities countless hours of travel and booking time and allowed them more time to patrol the streets of their cities.

Satellite Jail Closed

Shortly after the city of El Mirage terminated its contract with Sheriff Arpaio, the sheriff decided to "close" the satellite jail facility in Surprise, Arizona. The facility is only 1½ miles from El Mirage and is located at Bell and Dysart Roads.

The sheriff publicly claimed it was a "budget issue." It was only a coincidence that he "closed" the facility after El Mirage terminated his contract for police service.

The fact is this facility is actually the Maricopa County Sheriff's Office District 3 substation. Arpaio didn't actually "close" the facility as he publicly stated. He just stopped providing the service to El Mirage and the other northwest Valley cities. Aside from the satellite jail, the facility is the permanent workplace for deputies, detectives and supervisors.

Sheriff Joe Arpaio was well aware that his decision to discontinue accepting arrestees would have a direct impact on the El Mirage Police Department as well as the neighboring Peoria and Surprise Police Departments.

But, his decision to stop accepting arrestees had an even more devastating impact on smaller police departments like Wickenburg and Youngtown.

The officers from Wickenburg had a 107-mile round trip drive to the main jail. The Youngtown Police Department often had only one or two police officers on-duty during a shift. If the officer spent 2-3 hours booking a prisoner in downtown Phoenix, the other officer was left on their own to patrol the city or respond to emergencies. If only one officer was on-duty, the city was left without any police coverage.

The manner in which he made the change was typical of Joe Arpaio. He gave no advance notice. In his typical in-your-face style Arpaio told a reporter from the *Arizona Republic*, *"It's up to them to get their prisoners downtown. I've been doing it as a favor."*

Of course, the professional protocol would have been to call a meeting of the police chiefs whose departments would be affected by closing the satellite jail. He could have explained the reason for the closing and discussed alternatives with the chiefs.

That would have given the police chiefs a chance to make staffing adjustments or determine alternative policy issues regarding arrestees. Instead, Arpaio simply made an announcement that he was discontinuing the service. End of story.

Closed or Not Closed?

Interestingly enough, about 3 months after Sheriff Arpaio supposedly "closed" the satellite booking facility I was in the parking lot of the sheriff's District 3 substation at Bell and Dysart Roads. About 60 law enforcement officers and tactical units had gathered there to hold a briefing prior to serving some "high risk" gang-related search warrants in El Mirage.

I noticed that some Maricopa County Sheriff Detention Officers were loading up a group of prisoners into a sheriff's transport van.

Like most days, I was wearing my El Mirage Police uniform at that time. A Maricopa County Sheriff sergeant was standing nearby so I asked him what was going on with the prisoner transport. He said the prisoners were being transported to the main jail in downtown Phoenix for booking.

I mentioned to the sergeant that I thought they had "closed" the satellite facility. He informed me that they still use the facility for "their own" prisoners but they "closed" it to other agencies. He just looked at me apologetically and walked away.

The lack of cooperation from the Maricopa County Sheriff's Office continued for many months. It was frustrating but we learned to adapt as best we could. The lack of timely communication with the sheriff's office often caused us many hours of extra work.

I was learning some valuable lessons about the "character" of some the command staff of the Maricopa County Sheriff's Office.

****

CHAPTER 6

The Mishandled Investigations

As described earlier Police Chief Mike Frazier took over as head of the El Mirage Police Department in early October 2007. During his first week as chief, Frazier received a call from a top commander of the Maricopa County Sheriff's Office. The sheriff's commander informed Chief Frazier that the sheriff's office wanted to return several boxes of police reports to the El Mirage Police Department.

The police reports were mostly sex-crime investigations that occurred in El Mirage during the previous 2+ year period when the sheriff's office was under contract to provide police service. The commander from the sheriff's office told Chief Frazier that all the police reports were "completed investigations" and could just be "filed away."

Since the crimes had occurred in the city of El Mirage, Chief Frazier agreed that the police reports should be filed in the Police Records Section at the El Mirage Police Department. Frazier made arrangements to have the boxes of police reports picked up at the Maricopa County Sheriff's Office and returned to the El Mirage Police Department.

The Review

Normally, we might have taken the sheriff's commander at his word that the returned boxes of police reports were "completed investigations" and just filed them away. But, something just didn't seem right about the police reports from the sheriff's office. Had we done so, we might never have discovered the many cases that had been mishandled by the Maricopa County Sheriff's Special Victims Unit.

At that time we had already been reviewing the police reports on several death investigations the Maricopa County Sheriff's Office had handled while they were in El Mirage. The cases included murders, suicides and unexplained deaths. Some of the cases appeared to be incomplete, unfinished or improperly concluded.

So, with the knowledge of the poorly handled death investigations I ordered a review of the police reports contained in the boxes returned from the Maricopa County Sheriff's Office.

In November 2007 a detective from the "new" El Mirage Police Department began examining the boxed up police reports. A cursory review of those cases showed that most of the reports were incomplete.

Police Chief Mike Frazier called the deputy chief at the Maricopa County Sheriff's Office who had previously told Frazier the police reports were "complete" and ready to be filed away.

Frazier told him we had reviewed some of the police reports and they were actually *incomplete* investigations. The sheriff's deputy chief apologized to Frazier and offered to have the police reports returned to the sheriff's office where he would have detectives "complete the investigations."

Chief Frazier declined the offer. The victims of these crimes were El Mirage residents and the cases would be reviewed by the "new" El Mirage Police Department.

Based on our review of the sheriff's death investigations and the boxes of incomplete sex-crime cases, we had little confidence that these investigations would have been handled properly if returned to the Maricopa County Sheriff's Office.

As the El Mirage Police Department continued to review the cases it became very clear that many of the neglected cases returned by the sheriff's office were serious crimes and most were from their Special Victims Unit.

The El Mirage Detective Sergeant and his staff contacted their peers at the Maricopa County Sheriff's Office on several different occasions informing them of the apparent widespread neglect they had uncovered.

Each day as more detailed information about the neglected police reports emerged it was passed on from the El Mirage police to the sheriff's office. But, the sheriff's staff showed little enthusiasm about hearing the information. Within a few weeks, communication with the Maricopa County Sheriff's Office became extremely difficult for the El Mirage police staff.

Inappropriate Clearances

As we continued to review the El Mirage police reports returned to us from the Maricopa County Sheriff's Office we began to see another disturbing trend.

One of the El Mirage detectives first noticed it. Shortly thereafter, the Detective Sergeant began seeing it and mentioned it to me. Then I began to see it myself in the sheriff's police reports that I read.

The trend we were seeing was the frequent and inappropriate use of the term "Exceptionally Cleared" by sheriff's investigators as a classification to "close" a case. We found inappropriate "clearances" in Maricopa County Sheriff's Office reports on death investigations, sexual assaults, child molesting and other serious felony cases.

Crime Statistics

Most police agencies across the country use crime statistics to monitor crime in their jurisdiction. Responsible law enforcement agencies use these statistics to allocate manpower, direct resources and establish crime suppression goals. Politicians and community leaders often use crime statistics to measure the effectiveness of a police department or sheriff's office.

When crime statistics show that the crime rate has gone "up" in a community, the police chief or sheriff may be viewed as ineffective in suppressing crime in their jurisdiction. When the crime rate goes "down" law enforcement usually takes some of the credit and are viewed in a positive light.

Crime statistics are important to all police agencies. Equally important is the manner in which the statistics are tracked and reported. Manipulating or "cheating" on statistics can provide an inaccurate or inflated picture of the effectiveness of a police or sheriff department.

The Unified Crime Report (UCR)

The FBI created a reporting and tracking system to monitor crime statistics in the United States. It is known as the Uniform Crime Report (UCR). This system is used by nearly all police and sheriff agencies across the country. The theory of the system is to provide a *uniform* manner of capturing crime data throughout the United States. Therefore, it is essential that every law enforcement agency tracks their statistics in accordance with the "standard" established by the FBI.

One of the categories that the UCR statistics tracks is "clearances." To law enforcement leaders "clearances" are considered a "positive" because the term reflects crimes that have been "solved." The ratio of the number of crimes that occurred to the number of those crimes solved is known as the "Clearance Rate." (Example: 100 crimes occurred and 10 were solved = 10% "Clearance Rate.")

"Clearances Rates" are a very important statistic for law enforcement agencies. The management of a police department or sheriff's office often uses "Clearance Rates" to measure the effectiveness of its investigators.

According to the FBI standard there are only a few ways a law enforcement agency may legitimately close or "clear" a case. Basically, a crime remains open or unsolved until it is either "Cleared by Arrest" or "Exceptionally Cleared" (also known as "Cleared by Exception").

An agency can classify a case as "Cleared by Arrest" (CBA) only after a person has been arrested, charged with the commission of the offense and turned over to the court for prosecution.

A case can only be "Exceptionally Cleared" if elements *beyond law enforcement's control* prevent the agency from arresting and charging the offender. The FBI guidelines are strict and limit the use of "Exceptionally Cleared." Examples of "Exceptionally Cleared" cases include the death of the suspect before he could be charged or a victim's refusal to cooperate with prosecution *after* the suspect has been positively identified.

Maricopa County Sheriff's Office Cases

During our review of the Maricopa County Sheriff's Office police reports we saw a trend of inappropriate "clearances." It appeared that Maricopa County Sheriff's investigators were inappropriately "clearing" cases contrary to the established FBI's UCR protocol.

The sheriff's detectives were "clearing" many cases that did not fit the established criteria. This practice would easily inflate their "clearance rates" and shed an inaccurate light on their effectiveness.

After discussing this issue with Police Chief Mike Frazier I called the commander of the Maricopa County Sheriff's Office criminal investigations unit. *(It took numerous attempts but I eventually managed to speak with him on the phone.)* I told him about our review of their cases and the apparent problem with the "clearances" on the reports we reviewed.

The sheriff commander acknowledged an understanding of the UCR protocol but informed me that the sheriff's office doesn't "interpret" the standard the same way we did. I suggested to him that the inappropriate clearances skewed their statistics and did not accurately reflect crime in the county. After a few moments of "debate" the commander simply said, "That's the way we do it."

Based on our conversation it was obvious the Maricopa County Sheriff's Office had no intention of complying with the FBI's national UCR standards. And, of course, applying their own "interpretation" of the nationwide standard made the Sheriff's Office crime statistics look better. So, I simply ended our conversation.

I told Chief Frazier about my conversation with the sheriff's investigations commander. He was amazed that an agency as large as the Maricopa County Sheriff's Office would not follow the FBI standard. Both of us just shook our heads and let it go. Sheriff Joe Arpaio plays by his own rules.

The Mishandled Cases

Most of the mishandled sex-crime cases were now a few years old and any earlier investigative "leads" were probably "cold." Nonetheless, the El Mirage Police Department reviewed each report to see if any cases had "workable leads" or were still solvable.

On many occasions the El Mirage police supervisors asked the sheriff's investigators and supervisors if they had any more documentation on these cases. The responses from the Maricopa County Sheriff's Office were usually delayed by days and weeks. When they finally did reply their typical response was "no." They said the incomplete reports they gave to the El Mirage police were all they had.

El Mirage command staff took the word of the Maricopa County Sheriff's Office that they were not withholding any other documentation on these cases.

It was quite evident to us that the Maricopa County Sheriff's Office had mishandled dozens of serious child sex crimes. They failed to properly investigate or complete these felony investigations - most of which involved young children. Over the next several months the El Mirage Police Department expended vast resources re-investigating the cases they neglected.

By December 2007 it had become clear to the El Mirage Police Department that a serious problem existed in the Maricopa County Sheriff's Office Special Victims Unit. It was also clear that Sheriff Joe Arpaio and his command staff were now well aware of the problem.

Kool Aid Drinkers

This scandalous issue of mishandled sex-crime cases on the part of the Maricopa County Sheriff's Office was extensive and had to be addressed. For the sake of the many victims involved in these cases, the situation had to be handled properly and professionally. But, the lack of cooperation by Sheriff Joe Arpaio's staff made it difficult for those of us at the El Mirage Police Department.

But, I also knew that not all of Sheriff Joe Arpaio's top staff members were "Kool Aid drinkers." *(This was a reference we often made about the similarities between Sheriff Joe Arpaio's internal followers and the members of the Jonestown cult who blindly followed their cult leader Jim Jones and knowingly drank poisoned Kool Aid during a mass suicide in 1978.)*

Some of Arpaio's supervisors and top commanders refused to accept his poison and maintained their integrity. They were generally demonized within the organization and reassigned to obscure positions.

An even fewer number managed to not drink Arpaio's Kool Aid and still remained members of his inner sanctum. To do so was extremely risky and required them to play a constant game of charades.

During my 31 years of police work at the Phoenix Police Department I made many friends at the Maricopa County Sheriff's Office. I had worked alongside many of the deputies, supervisors and top commanders of the

M.C.S.O. Some of them turned their backs on our friendship when I went to work at El Mirage.

But, others kept their relationship with me "silently" alive. Amazingly, our friendship and working relationship had to be kept secret. If Arpaio ever found out they were even communicating with me there would have been severe repercussions for them by the sheriff or his top henchman Dave Hendershott. Talking or sharing information with me would have been considered "collaborating with the enemy."

Secret Meetings

Sheriff Joe Arpaio and Chief Deputy Dave Hendershott blatantly refused to allow his staff to cooperate with the El Mirage Police Department. As a result I had to "secretly" contact my trustworthy confidants within the sheriff's office.

These face-to-face meetings were like something out of a Mafia movie. As amazing it may sound I could *never* contact them on their county phones. I always had to call them on their personal cell phones. If we were to meet in person, I had to be in "plainclothes" and drive an unmarked police car. We had to meet at a location 20 miles or more from El Mirage and nowhere near any Maricopa County facility. For them to be seen with me would be "career suicide."

Regardless, the magnitude of the mishandled sex-crime cases compelled me to reach out to one of my confidants at the Maricopa County Sheriff's Office. I first discussed the situation with my boss Chief Frazier. I told him I was going to arrange one of my "secret" meetings to discuss the mishandled sex-crimes cases. Frazier agreed it was an important issue that needed to be discussed. We needed confirmation that the Maricopa County Sheriff's Office was not withholding any documentation about the mishandled police reports.

Chief Frazier and I also agreed that it was absurd that high-level police professionals had to operate under these "secret" conditions. But, such was the workplace environment created by Sheriff Joe Arpaio.

It took several days but I finally arranged a covert meeting with one of my sheriff's office confidants. I told him it was important that we meet to talk about the dozens of mishandled sex-crime cases that had been returned to us from the sheriff's office. He was already aware of the problem with the police reports and agreed to meet with me.

I had to be careful not to betray the confidence my remaining friends at the Maricopa County Sheriff's Office had in me. I did not want them to fall prey to Sheriff Arpaio's retaliation for communicating with me.

As usual we met in plainclothes at an obscure location many miles from where either of us worked. But the meeting turned out to be worthwhile.

During our covert meeting the high ranking sheriff's officer disclosed in confidence that Sheriff Arpaio's office recognized they had a widespread problem of neglect in their Special Victims Unit. He said it wasn't just in the cases from El Mirage but was county-wide. The officer said it would be "prudent" for the El Mirage Police Department to look into these cases as they were in all likelihood never completed by the Special Victims Unit.

I told him that we planned to spend a lot of time and resources re-investigating the mishandled cases. I needed verification that the Maricopa County Sheriff's Office was not withholding any documentation on these cases. He said the reports they gave to us were all they had.

Finally, based on the information I got through this "secret" meeting we now had the confirmation we needed to move forward.

The Sheriff's Reaction

During our clandestine meeting the sheriff's commander told me that Sheriff Arpaio was "very concerned" about how the El Mirage Police Department was going to handle this scandal and if we planned to "go public" with the information. Listening to the commander describe the sheriff's reaction it appeared that Sheriff Arpaio was more concerned about bad publicity than the dozens of victims in El Mirage whose cases were neglected.

I told him that we had no intention of disclosing any information about the mishandled cases. We did intend to look into the cases and "re-open" any investigations that appeared to have workable leads.

I told the commander that Chief Frazier and I had discussed how Sheriff Arpaio might react to this scandal and the bad publicity it was sure to bring. I told him that Chief Frazier and I had even discussed our concerns that Arpaio would order his troops to serve a search warrant on the El Mirage Police Department to seize our records on the mishandled cases. *(Chief Frazier and I both agreed it would be outrageous for Arpaio to do so but not beyond the realm of possibility.)*

Even though I knew he wouldn't tell me, I asked my confidant if the Sheriff was planning a raid on the El Mirage Police Department to seize our records. He gave me a funny look and didn't respond.

Clearly, it would have been improper for him to disclose to me whether they planned a raid so he never did answer the question. But his reaction led me to believe that seizing the El Mirage Police Department records had been discussed by the Maricopa County Sheriff's upper echelon.

After talking for an hour or so my friend from the sheriff's office agreed that the El Mirage Police Department was dealing with the situation of the mishandled police reports correctly. He wished me luck; we shook hands and once again went our separate ways.

I returned to El Mirage later that day and briefed Chief Frazier about what I had learned. It was clear that the Maricopa County Sheriff's Office was fully aware of the mishandled sex-crime cases.

(Note: The El Mirage Police Department spent the next several months quietly reviewing the neglected police reports and re-investigating those cases with investigative leads. The scandal was only made public several months later when investigative reporters from the *Arizona Republic* and *East Valley Tribune* finally uncovered the mistakes made by the sheriff's office by reviewing public records.)

****

SECTION TWO

The Police Reports

<u>Chapters</u>

7 – Internet and Chat Room Dangers
(3 police reports)

8 – Runaway Juveniles (2 police reports)

9 – Child Molesters and Pedophiles
(5 police reports)

10 – Live-in Boyfriends, Step-fathers and House guests
(5 police reports)

11 - Fathers Who Molest Their Biological Children
(5 police reports)

12 – Sexual Assaults (6 police reports)

13 – Other Sex Crimes Against Children
(5 police reports)

The Police Reports

Goals of the Book

There are two clear goals for this book. The first is to provide a first-hand account of the mishandled sex crimes cases that happened in El Mirage under Sheriff Joe Arpaio's watch. The victims in all 31 cases examined in this book were children and young teens.

The second goal is to produce an educational tool for child sex-crimes prevention. This book examines the real life dangers that our children face from sexual predators in various aspects of everyday life. With the use of actual police reports readers get an in-depth look at the "real life" situations of the victims and exactly what led to them being molested, sexually assaulted or exploited.

Many young people often confuse *reality* with *Reality TV*. The differences between real life and what they see on television is staggering. Reality sometimes results in hard lessons as described in the police reports in this book.

The mishandling of hundreds of sex-crime cases by the Maricopa County Sheriff's Office is an inexcusable miscarriage of justice. But, if parents and kids can use the tragic experiences of the victims in this book to avoid becoming victims themselves, then perhaps something positive will be achieved.

31 Mishandled Cases

The following chapters of this book contain police reports from the El Mirage Police Department. The review of these cases provides the reader with specific information on 31 sex crimes that were reported by the victims, but subsequently mishandled by the Maricopa County Sheriff's Office in El Mirage. Nearly every one of the 31 cases involves children.

The El Mirage Police Department found dozens of other cases that had been mishandled by the sheriff's office. News accounts put the number of mishandled cases throughout Maricopa County at over 400. But, this book focuses on 31 police reports of Sexual Assault, Child Molesting and Sexual Misconduct With a Minor – all victims from the small city of El Mirage, Arizona.

The criminal cases described in the pages ahead provide insight into what actually happened to the child victims in El Mirage. As the reader you will get a chance to see exact details about the crimes and how the cases were investigated – and subsequently mishandled. Following each police report is a brief summary detailing how the case should have been handled properly.

Other local news publications such as the *East Valley Tribune* and *The New Times* have published factual articles highlighting some of the other cases from El Mirage. The cases contained in this book are some of the serious yet "less publicized" crimes that were mishandled by Maricopa County Sheriff Joe Arpaio's Office.

Categories:

The circumstances surrounding the victims of the 31 reported crimes listed in this book are broken into seven different categories:

- Internet and Chat Room Dangers (3 reports)
- Runaway Juveniles (2 reports)
- Child Molesters and Pedophiles (5 reports)
- "Live-in" boyfriends, step-fathers, house guests (5 reports)
- Fathers who molest their biological children (5 reports)
- Sexual assaults (6 reports)
- Other sex crimes against children (5 reports)

The 31 police reports included in this book contain specific details based on information taken directly from the police reports. The original police reports were written by the police officers and deputies who were at the scene. Most of the case reviews contain direct quotes from victims as they describe their ordeal to the police.

The case summaries have been written in the "real world" police format that officers use every day. However, much of the "cop lingo" from the police reports has been converted to everyday rhetoric for ease of reading. The content of the police reports has been summarized and paraphrased in each case review.

The following chapters also include detailed information about each of the seven categories listed above. The book describes the hazards children encounter when they run away from home and cites some of the reasons kids go missing. There is specific information about the dangers children face using the Internet and tips for parents to better supervise their kids' use of the Internet.

Information on pedophiles and other child predators is included to provide the reader with a better understanding of how dangerous these offenders can be. Also included is information about the root causes most commonly associated with the molesting of young girls by "live-in" boyfriends, step-fathers, family members and friends.

The following chapters also include profiles and studies on biological fathers who molest their children, rapists and other sexual deviants.

The Victims:

An analysis of the victims in the 31 police reports described in this book shows there were 35 total victims. (Note: Some of the 31 crime reports list multiple victims.) Ninety-five percent of the victims were female and all were under the age of 18 years. Twenty-eight of the victims (80%) were age 14 or younger. The race of the victims was approximately 43% White, 43% Hispanic, 11% Black and 3% Asian.

VICTIMS

TOTAL VICTIMS
35

GENDER/RACE

Male

2

(5%)

White	Hispanic
1	1

Female

33

(95%)

White	Hispanic	Black	Asian
14	14	4	1

AGE

Male

1-5 yrs	11-14 yrs
1	1

Female

1-5 yrs	6-10 yrs	11-14 yrs	15-17 yrs
5	6	15	7

ETHNICITY

WHITE	HISPANIC	BLACK	ASIAN
15	15	4	1
(42.8%)	(42.8%)	(11.6%)	(2.8%)

The Suspects:

The 31 suspects listed in this book were identified or described by their victims. Below is a breakdown of the suspects based on the information from the police reports. Nearly all the suspects were male - the only reported female suspect/s listed was from a juvenile group home where some teenage girls may have been sexually molesting some of the younger girls. The race of the suspects shows a slightly higher number of Hispanic vs. White suspects. While there was only one very young offender, nearly half (46%) of the suspects were over 30 years old, and 77% were over the age of 18 years. Adult males clearly make up the vast majority of the offenders in the 31 cases reviewed.

SUSPECTS

TOTAL SUSPECTS
31

GENDER

Male	Female
30	1
(96.8%)	(3.2%)

RACE/ETHNICITY

WHITE	HISPANIC	BLACK	NATIVE AMERICAN	UNKNOWN
12	14	2	1	2
(38.7%)	(45.3%)	(6.4%)	(6.4%)	(3.2%)

AGE

UNK	10 OR YOUNGER	11-17	18-20	21-29	30+
1	1	5	5	5	14
(3.2%)	(3.2%)	(16.1%)	(16.1%)	(16.1%)	(45.3%)

Privacy

Everything contained in the case reviews is based on the content of the actual police reports. The names of the victims, witnesses and suspects have all been changed to protect their privacy. No specific addresses of private residences are listed in the case summaries. Other literary steps have been taken to prevent anyone with evil intent from tracking down victims or witnesses.

The true names of most of the law enforcement officials listed in this book have been changed or omitted. Many of the officers, supervisors and commanders are still working in law enforcement in the metro Phoenix area. Some have expressed concerns over retaliation by the Maricopa County Sheriff's Office for sharing their insight, opinions or views of the operations of the sheriff's office.

But each case is real and taken directly from the factual El Mirage Police Department reports.

Current Status of 31 Mishandled Cases

When the El Mirage Police Department first received the mishandled cases from the by the sheriff's office in November 2007, some of the investigations were already more than two years old. The chances of salvaging these cases were slim. But, the El Mirage Police Department was determined to make a reasonable effort to locate the victims and bring their offenders to justice.

The mishandled cases were assigned to El Mirage detectives. These investigators spent the next several months tracking down victims, witnesses and/or their families.

Their investigative efforts revealed the following:

- Some cases had workable leads and were actively investigated.
- Several victims had moved from the address listed in the police report and left no forwarding address or phone number.
- Other victims felt too much time had elapsed and they no longer wanted to pursue their case.
- A few victims said they just wanted to "put the incident behind them."
- Some victims had gone through counseling and did not want to open an "old wound."
- A few victims had new relationships in their lives and did not want their past disclosed.

It is important to note that in early 2012 the Maricopa County Attorney announced that his office was reviewing hundreds of cases mishandled by the Maricopa County Sheriff's Office to see if any could still be prosecuted. As a precaution, the *current status* of the 31 investigations in this book were omitted. This was done primarily:

- To avoid jeopardizing any on-going investigation or prosecution.
- To avoid alerting the offender that a particular case is still active.
- To protect the privacy of the victims and their family.

Disclaimer:

A review of the El Mirage police reports listed in this book showed these cases were clearly mishandled by the Maricopa County Sheriff's Office. Most of the cases had been assigned to their Special Victims Unit.

The conclusions stated in the following chapters that the cases were "incomplete" or mishandled is based on the in-depth review of the cases by the El Mirage Police Department and confirmation by a high ranking Maricopa County Sheriff's official.

Reasonable explanations for some of the shortcomings in these reports may exist. But no explanations were ever provided to the El Mirage Police Department after repeated requests. Their standard response: "That's all we have."

A top executive from the Maricopa County Sheriff's Office disclosed in confidence that they recognized they had a widespread problem of neglect in their Special Victims Unit.

WARNING:

Some of the material contained in these reports may not be appropriate for children or those who may be offended by foul language. Most of the reports also include graphic descriptions of what the victims told the police happened to them.

The case summaries are based on actual crime reports of *Sexual Assault, Child Molesting* and *Sexual Misconduct with a Minor*. Nearly all of them deal with victims who were under the age of 18 years. Most of them deal with young girls who were victimized by acquaintances, family members or complete strangers. The reports contain excerpts and specific quotes from victims and witnesses.

Cops are exposed to this type of language on a daily basis. Nonetheless, readers are warned that these summaries contain some unedited and specific quotes they may find offensive.

Chapter 7

Internet and "Chat Room" Dangers

Chapter 7 includes *three* police reports in which the children were sexually victimized by adults they met on the Internet or in Chat Rooms. The victims of these crimes were all girls between the ages of 12 and 15 years. These police reports were among the dozens of cases mishandled by the Maricopa County Sheriff's Office.

Also included is anecdotal information about the dangers our children face with the Internet and Chat Rooms. The chapter offers suggestions to parents on ways to protect their children when using their computers.

El Mirage Police Report

CASE #07-1050831
Sexual Misconduct With a Minor
Date: April 11, 2007
Victims: 13 and 14 year-old girls
Suspect: 22 and 24 year-old males

This case involves two young girls ages 13 and 14 years old. These two girls met two men in their mid-20's on a social website on the Internet. Unbeknownst to their parents the girls agreed to meet the men in person. A meeting was arranged at a grocery store and the girls foolishly got into a car with the two men. They ended up at local park, took illegal drugs and ended up having sex with the men.

Here is the police report:

Facts of the Case:

On April 11, 2006 an El Mirage police officer was dispatched on a call reference a Sexual Assault. The officer contacted the victim's aunt "Annabelle" and later the victim's mother "Paula."

Annabelle told the officer that her niece "Lisa" and her friend "Krystal" had met two men on-line using the social network MySpace. Lisa is 14 years old and Krystal is 13 years old. The men were 22 and 24 years-old.

After "chatting" with the men on the website both girls agreed to meet the men and ended up at a park in El

Mirage, Arizona. Annabelle said that when they got to the park the men offered the two young girls some illegal drugs. She said all four of them ingested the drugs by smoking.

Annabelle said that sometime after taking the drugs the men asked Lisa and Krystal to have sex with them. From what Annabelle was told both girls consented and engaged in sexual acts with the men.

According to Annabelle, the next morning Lisa's parents found out what happened and they took her to a Phoenix area hospital for an examination. Annabelle said they were also attempting to get Lisa some counseling over the incident.

The officer asked Annabelle if she knew the e-mail addresses of the two men. She said she did not have that information; but, the girls apparently knew it but were not telling her.

The officer later spoke with Lisa's mother Paula. She said she had more specific information about what had happened between her daughter and the two men. Lisa and her friend Krystal did, in fact, meet the two men on the Internet social network MySpace. She said the girls had been "chatting" with the men and exchanging e-mails.

They eventually agreed to meet the men in the parking lot of a grocery store near Cotton Lane and Waddell Road in Surprise, Arizona. From there the men drove the girls to a park in El Mirage. After doing some drugs the girls engaged in sex acts with the men. Around 10:00 p.m. the men dropped both girls off at a friend's house in Surprise, Arizona.

On the day all this occurred, Paula said she did not know Lisa's whereabouts so she called the Surprise Police Department. Paula said the police filed a Missing Persons/Runaway Juvenile report on Lisa. The information on Lisa was put into the nationwide law enforcement database N.C.I.C.

Paula said the next day she began searching for her daughter. She eventually located both Lisa and Krystal at the home of another friend in Surprise, Arizona.

Paula said she questioned Lisa and demanded to know where she had been. That's when Lisa disclosed the information about the two men she met on the Internet. When Paula heard Lisa had sex with one of the men she took her daughter to the hospital for an examination.

(Note: While the police report indicates Annabelle told the officer both girls had consensual sex with the men, there is no specific information in the report confirming whether Krystal did engage in sex with the men. The report does indicate that Lisa admitted to having sex with one of them.)

Paula told the officer that the girls refused to give up any more information about the suspects or their email addresses. They did not want the men to get in trouble.

Paula indicated that she did want these men prosecuted. The officer told her the case would be turned over to the detectives for follow up investigation.

The officer completed his report and turned it in to his sergeant. According to the police report the case was forwarded to the Maricopa County Sheriff's Office Special Victims Unit for follow up.

Findings of the El Mirage Police Review

This was a very disturbing case that has all the signs of adult child-predators using the Internet to lure vulnerable young girls. The two men clearly took advantage of these two runaways. The case certainly warranted immediate follow up investigation by detectives.

It shouldn't matter if the girls refused to give up the identities or e-mail information about the suspects. Their parents had the legal right to take the computers from their minor daughters and turn them over to the police. The detectives could have also obtained a search warrant to seize the computers and access the e-mail information.

While the 13 and 14 year-old girls may have consented to have sex with these adult men, they are still victims of sexual misconduct and protected under the law. Every effort should have been made to track down these suspects.

However, the report indicates that nothing more was done with this investigation by the Special Victims Unit. Based on the information given to the El Mirage Police Department it appears that the sheriff's office did not work this case and it was returned to El Mirage in 2007.

There is no information in the Maricopa County Sheriff's report that explains why this case was not worked by their Special Victims Unit.

Internet Dangers

Ever since the proliferation of the Internet, law enforcement officials have been warning parents and educators of the dangers lurking out there on the Internet and "Chat Rooms." Studies have been published regarding child-predators and other sexual deviants who prey on innocent children on the Internet.

Many organizations across the country provide tips for making children aware of the dangers on the Internet. Parents can follow these guidelines and coach their kids to stay away from suspicious online strangers. The guidelines include staying "private" while online and using parental control software. But, just as important, parents should discuss the tactics used by on-line predators and the dangers they pose. Parents should be open and honest with their younger children and teens about the dangers lurking on the Internet.

It should never be a surprise to parents as to which websites their children are accessing or who they are chatting with on the Internet. There is "Parental Protection" software available for parents to monitor the activities of their children on the Internet. But, somehow the message has not gotten through to all parents.

It's a good idea for parents to have a discussion with their kids about which social networking sites they use. Parents should have them access the site in front of them to see for themselves that its safe and age-appropriate. Some sites have built-in protections or age limit restrictions. For example, most parents don't realize that MySpace doesn't allow access to kids under 14 years old - but the site doesn't verify a kids' age.

Parents should check their child's "profile" on a social network site to see whether they have listed only appropriate information about themselves. If a parent wants to delete a site from their child's computer they simply contact the social networking site directly.

Parents should explain to their children that it is dangerous to post their full name, address, phone number, school name or any other personal information that would allow an unwanted person to find them.

Photographs that kids post on the Internet can often reveal personal information if they're not careful. It's just not a safe practice for children to send photos to strangers they meet online.

Parents should also familiarize themselves about "Privacy Settings" on the social websites. These settings control who their kids allow to view their personal information and profiles.

One of the most important rules a parent can insist upon is that their children <u>never</u> agree to meet anyone in person they meet on the Internet. Parents should explain to their kids that people met on the Internet are not always who they say they are.

Proper and effective parental supervision of kids on the Internet is the best way to keep them safe from Internet predators and stalkers. One of the basic tenets of Internet safety is the location of the child's computer. Parents should only allow the computer to be used in a common area of their home.

Today's children and their use of the Internet and text messaging has created an entire language of codes and shorthand. Parents can access different websites that explain the lingo that children use to communicate on their different devices. Parents want to be aware of messages such as *"POS"* (parent over shoulder) and *"LMIRL"* (let's meet in real life).

Parents should tell their kids that it's important to notify them immediately if they are ever <u>solicited for sex on-line</u>. **Those types of solicitations should be reported to the local police immediately.**

Despite all the warnings about the dangers of the Internet, children are still being victimized by Internet predators at an alarming rate. But, these crimes usually have many workable leads that law enforcement can follow to locate and arrest these deviant offenders.

But, only if the law enforcement agency handles the investigation properly.

El Mirage Police Report

CASE #06-1122104
Sexual Assault
January 3, 2006
Victim: 12-year old female
Suspect: Three older teenage males

This incident deals with two young girls, ages 11 and 12, who spent the night at a friend's house in Phoenix. The girls got on a "chat line" and met some older boys who were in their late teens. Later that night the boys drove to the house and the 11 and 12 year-old girls left with them in a car. The girls were driven to a house in El Mirage and held against their will. One or both of the girls engaged in sex with the teenage boys and were later dropped off back in Phoenix.

Here is the police report:

Facts of the Case:

On January 3, 2006 at around 2:00 p.m. a deputy from the Maricopa County Sheriff's Office was dispatched to Phoenix area hospital in reference to a Sexual Assault of two juvenile females. The deputy learned that the incident had occurred at a home in El Mirage near 129th Ave. & Peoria Ave.

The staff from the hospital briefed the deputy about what the victim and her mother told them had occurred. They originally believed that the two young girls had been assaulted but it appears that the younger 11-year old girl was not harmed.

The deputy then spoke with the 12-year old victim's mother "Maria." She told the deputy that her daughter "Valerie" was supposed to spend the night at the home of her friend "Cathy." According to Maria, Cathy is 15 years old and they have known each other for quite a while. A neighbor friend named "Missy" (age 11) was also spending the night with the girls at Cathy's apartment near 71st & Campbell Avenues in Phoenix.

Maria said yesterday evening Cathy and her brother picked up Valerie and Missy at her home in a black car and they first went to one of the local shopping malls. After hanging out at the mall for a while the girls all went to Cathy's apartment. According to Maria, Missy made a phone call from the apartment (maybe to a "party line"). A short while later three older teenage males showed up in a silver car. Valerie and Missy met the guys in the parking lot and left with them in the car.

Maria told the deputy that her daughter Valerie told her that they drove around for a while and ended up at a "white house" in El Mirage near 129th Ave. & Peoria Ave. Valerie did not know the exact address. Maria said that Valerie told her she became frightened and tried to call her mom but the teenage males wouldn't let her call.

Valerie told her mother that the guys took her into another room and "pressured" her into having sex with one of them. Maria said that her daughter told her that the teenagers told her they would "hurt her" if she told anybody what happened. Valerie said she believed the males were all 17 or 18 years old and she only knew their first names.

According to Valerie, nothing happened to 11-year old Missy and the teenagers did not touch or harm her.

The older male teenagers later drove Valerie and Missy back to the area of Cathy's apartment and dropped them at a park near 73rd Ave. & Campbell Ave. Valerie used the cell phone of one of the teenagers and called her mother. (Note: The phone number was not blocked. Maria saved the cell phone number and gave it to the deputy as a lead to track down the suspects.)

Maria told the deputy she was concerned about what happened to her daughter so she took her to the hospital and called the police. She told the deputy she would assist in prosecuting the suspects.

The deputy next talked to "Antonia" who is Missy's mother. Antonia related to the deputy that her daughter told her she had planned to go with some friends to a nearby shopping mall in Phoenix. Antonia told her daughter to be home by 7:00 p.m.

Missy told her mother that her friend Cathy and her brother picked her up at home and drove to the mall. Afterwards they went to Cathy's apartment. Antonia said that Missy told her that she called "some guys" who came and picked them up at Cathy's apartment complex. Missy told her mother that the guys "forced them" to go with them in their car. She said they told her they would "hurt them" if they didn't go.

Antonia said her daughter told her the males took them to a house near 125th Ave. & Peoria Ave. in El Mirage. Missy told her mother that she was taken to a dark room where she waited. According to Antonia, her daughter said no one touched her or hurt her. Antonia told the deputy she will assist in prosecuting the males who took her daughter.

Antonia told the deputy her daughter was supposed to be home around 7:00 p.m. When she didn't come home she got worried and started looking for Missy. Around 10:30 p.m. she called Maria to see if she knew where the girls were. She found out Missy and Valerie were spending the night at Cathy's house. The next morning she found out what happened. She took her daughter to the hospital and called the police.

Next, the deputy interviewed "Kim" the hospital triage nurse. Kim said she talked to both the girls about what had happened.

The nurse told the deputy that 12-year old Valerie told her that she and her 11-year old friend Missy had spent the night at a friend's house. Kim said the girls told her they made a call and some teenage guys came over and "took them" to a house in El Mirage. She said that Valerie told her she "wanted to go home" but the guys wouldn't let her go. Kim told the deputy that Valerie told her she was taken into a room with one of the males whom Valerie believed was 17 years old. Valerie also told the nurse that Missy was alone in another room with an 18-year old male.

Kim told the deputy that Missy told her after they went to the mall they went back to Cathy's apartment and Cathy made a call on a "party line." She said that some time later some teenage guys came by and picked them up. Missy told the nurse that she did not have sex and no one touched her. She said she fell asleep on a couch in a large open room. Missy said when she woke up Valerie was in a room with three teenage guys. According to Missy, Valerie came out of the room and told Missy the guys said they would kill them if she or Missy told anyone what happened.

The nurse told the sheriff's deputy that Valerie appeared to be deceptive by the way she talked to her. She believed something did happen but that Valerie may also be hiding something.

According to the sheriff deputy's report he notified the Maricopa County Sheriff's Office Special Victims Unit and two detectives arrived at the hospital to take over the investigation.

Findings of the El Mirage Police Review

Although the police report indicates that Special Victims Unit detectives went to the hospital to take over this case, there is no documentation showing the investigation was ever completed.

In January 2008 the case was re-assigned to an investigator from the "new" El Mirage Police Department. A review of the facts indicate this case clearly needed further investigation. More than likely something did happen to these two young girls. They may have been culpable for putting themselves in a dangerous situation.

However, whether or not these young girls were actually taken or held against their will is only secondary if the older teenage males had sex with them. Consensual or not, sexual relations with an 11 or 12-year old child is a Class 2 felony in Arizona.

The information in the police report indicates this was clearly a prosecutable case and warranted further follow up by the Special Victims Unit detectives.

Law Enforcement's Response to Internet Predators

Law enforcement has stepped up and met the challenge of these Internet stalkers who prey on innocent children. Millions of law enforcement dollars have been poured into technology and training of law enforcement officers. New advances in computer technology create difficulty for law enforcement to track Internet predators and trace them to their computers. Advanced training in computer forensic examinations has allowed the officers to stay ahead of the technology curve.

The FBI created a national task force known as the Internet Crimes Against Children Task Force (ICAC) to combat child predators that use the Internet to stalk their prey. It's a cooperative effort between the FBI and local law enforcement with individual task forces located in all the major cities including Phoenix.

The task force program was created as the number of children and teenagers using the Internet began to increase. As on-line activity by kids increased so did the activity by predators. Law enforcement had to respond effectively and the ICAC Task Force was formed.

The ICAC program encompasses a network of more than 60 task forces with more than 2,000 federal, state, and local law enforcement agencies. The activities of the ICAC Task Forces include pro-active investigations, forensic examination of computers and criminal prosecutions. The ICAC program has helped local law enforcement agencies develop effective, responses to online child victimization. ICAC investigations have resulted in the arrest of more than 30,000 suspects since its inception in 1998.

Today, most Internet crimes involving sexual predators are solvable - that is, if they are properly investigated by the law enforcement agency.

El Mirage Police Report

CASE #07-1122108
Sexual Exploitation of a Minor
July 12, 2007
Victim: 15 year-old female
Suspect: Unknown age male

This case involved an unsuspecting 15 year-old girl who met a man on-line who told her he was also 15 years-old. In all likelihood he is an adult sexual predator. He spent months chatting with the girl and eventually gained her confidence. The girl ended up doing things she will likely regret the rest of her life.

Here is the police report:

Facts of the Case:

On July 12, 2007 around 11:30 a.m. a Maricopa County Sheriff's deputy was dispatched to a residence in the 12800 block of West Rosewood Drive on a radio call. The Maricopa County Sheriff's Office was under contract to provide police service to El Mirage so a sheriff's deputy was summoned to do the investigation.

When the deputy arrived at the house he contacted the 15 year-old victim who identified herself as "Alexis" and her parents "Sundi" and "Lester."

Alexis explained to the deputy the reason she had called the police. She said she had sent some nude pictures of herself via e-mail to a guy she met on-line who said his name was "Evan." She also gave the deputy Evan's e-mail address where she sent the photos. The deputy included the e-mail address in his report.

Alexis said she never met Evan in person but he told her he was 15 years old and lived in Texas. (Note: In reality there is no way to know his real name or true age. Internet stalkers and child predators often lie on-line about their age to lure in younger girls.)

She told the deputy she first met Evan on-line in an Internet chat room in March 2007. Alexis provided the deputy with the website of the chat room for his report. They continued to communicate via Internet, e-mail and chat rooms for a few weeks.

She said they later exchanged telephone numbers and began talking on the phone as well. Alexis gave the deputy the phone number she used to call Evan. The 15 year-old Alexis said they developed what she felt was a close relationship with Evan though she never met him in person.

Then sometime in April 2007 Alexis said Evan began pressuring her to send him nude photos of herself. Alexis said she refused and Evan continued to pressure her but she wouldn't send any photos.

Evan then broke off the relationship because Alexis refused to send him nude photos of herself. Alexis said a day later she agreed to send him a photo because she didn't want to end their relationship.

With her mother's camera Alexis took a picture of herself from the waist up with her bare breasts exposed. She sent the photo to Evan at the e-mail address she gave the deputy. Alexis said that Evan seemed happy that she sent the picture but he soon began pressuring her to send more explicit nude photos of herself.

When Alexis refused to send any more pictures, Evan threatened to post the first nude photo of Alexis on the Internet if she didn't send more pictures. He also told her if she didn't comply with his demands he would send the photo to her parents and distribute the picture around her school.

Alexis said she was afraid Evan would carry out his threats so she complied and sent him three more nude pictures which she took with her mother's digital camera phone. She described the first picture was of her naked vaginal area and the second of her buttocks. For the third photo, Alexis said she placed the camera on the floor and took a picture exposing her totally nude body. She said she loaded the three pictures onto her computer and sent them to Evan at the same e-mail address.

Alexis provided the deputy with a printed copy of an e-mail between her and Evan that occurred on July 6, 2007. In the e-mail, Evan admitted he was blackmailing Alexis. He told her she had to keep sending him nude photos of herself "until he decided she could stop."

Alexis said that at that point she was terrified. So, she told her parents about the situation and they called the police.

Alexis told the deputy she did not want to send any of the photos but she was afraid Evan would distribute her first photo at school. She said she didn't like sending the pictures and "cried the whole time" she was doing it.

Between July 9 and 10, 2007 Alexis received four e-mails messages in her personal hotmail account. All four e-mails were from strangers who said they had "seen her photos on a website." Alexis gave the deputy the e-mail addresses from the four messages.

Alexis's mother said they would not assist in prosecution. She said they wanted the police to contact Evan and just tell him to stop. The victim and her family are of Asian descent and her mother believed exposing what Alexis had done would bring great shame to their family.

Regardless of whether the victim's mother wanted to prosecute, the deputy recognized this was a very serious crime and notified his supervisor. The sergeant notified the Computer Crimes Division and Special Victims Unit.

The deputy obtained copies of all the e-mail messages, the email addresses, websites and other correspondence from Alexis' computer and impounded them as evidence. He completed his report and turned it in to his supervisor.

His report indicates that a copy of the report was sent to the Special Victims Unit for further investigation.

The following day a detective from the El Mirage Police Department served a search warrant on Alexis' home and seized her computer. The computer was impounded as evidence. A forensic examination would be done to retrieve the photos, emails and all other items of evidence to further the investigation.

Findings of the El Mirage Police Review

The responding deputy recognized this was a very serious case of Sexual Exploitation of a Minor involving a dangerous Internet predator. This 15 year-old girl had been victimized and was now being blackmailed. Nude photos of the girl had apparently been posted on a website against her will.

This case clearly warranted immediate further investigation by detectives. Law enforcement personnel today have the knowledge, expertise and technical capability to solve these Internet crimes effectively. The information provided in the deputy's initial report provided many leads to begin the investigation. This Internet predator needed to be tracked down, identified and stopped.

However, a review of this report revealed nothing beyond the responding deputy's initial report. The sheriff's report does not include any explanation as to why the case was not completed.

How Child Predators Use the Internet

Child predators on the Internet have become very sophisticated in the different ways they lure in their victims. They "hang around" teenage chat rooms and monitor what the kids are saying to each other. They often pick up nuances or clues that indicate that a child is vulnerable. They monitor and keep track of the likes and dislikes that kids chat about over the Internet.

Detectives from the Phoenix Police Department conducted a 6-month investigation on an Internet stalker. The suspect was a convicted sex offender with a record for Sexual Misconduct With a Minor involving a 13 year-old girl. He was 38 years old man and was posing as a 16 year-old boy and a familiar persona in various teenage "chat rooms" on the Internet. At the conclusion of the investigation, the Phoenix detectives served a search warrant on the suspect's home. They seized his computer and all related materials as evidence to prosecute him. Within the items seized they found computer logs he had created with the "chat" names of more than 25 kids he had been monitoring. The logs contained the likes, dislikes and personal information which the kids had unsuspectingly divulged in the "chat rooms."

Predators often use fake names and create "personas" as juveniles in order to lure these children into a false sense of security. Some predators will take long periods of time - weeks and even months to gain the trust and confidence of children and make them believe he is their friend. All the while the predator is gathering information about the child which he will use to somehow enter their life and eventually victimize them.

Young girls sometimes talk about their relationships and divulge in "chat rooms" if they had a recent break-up with their boyfriend. An Internet stalker will capitalize on that information and may strike up a conversation with the girl. He may spend weeks or even months saying things to her which make her feel good about herself, forget about the break-up and become attracted to him.

Most reported Internet predator crimes can be solved and the suspects arrested – *if the case is handled correctly by the investigating agency.*

****

Chapter 8

Runaway Juveniles

Chapter 8 includes *two* police reports in which juveniles ran away from home and were subsequently sexually victimized by adults. The victims of these crimes were girls between the ages of 15 and 16 years. These police reports were among the dozens of cases mishandled by the Maricopa County Sheriff's Office.

This chapter also includes information about the dangers children are exposed to when they run away from home. Also included is information for parents, teachers and counselors about runaway prevention, the distinction between a "Missing Person" and a "Runaway Juvenile," and the reasons young people run away from home.

El Mirage Police Report

CASE # 07-1050830
Sexual Assault
Date: April 27, 2007
Victim: 16 year-old female
Suspect: 30 year-old male

This case involves a 16 year-old girl who ran away from home and was associating with other runaways and drug users. One night she was at the home of one of her girlfriends along with several other people. A 30 year-old man who was also at the house accused her of stealing some drugs from him. He took the young girl into a back bedroom of the house where he beat and forcibly raped her.

Here is the police report:

Facts of the Case:

On March 27, 2007 a Maricopa County Sheriff's deputy was dispatched to a Phoenix Hospital in reference to a Sexual Assault. Phoenix Police officers had originally responded to the call at the hospital but determined that the crime actually occurred in the city of El Mirage. The Maricopa County Sheriff's Office was under contract to provide police service to El Mirage so a sheriff's deputy was summoned to do the investigation.

When the deputy arrived the Phoenix Police officers told him the rape victim's name was "Melanie" and she was a 16 year-old runaway from Phoenix. They told the deputy that Melanie said she was raped inside a house in El Mirage by a 30 year-old Native American man named "Sun Sinsoho." The officer said Melanie did not have an exact address where it occurred but the house belongs to a friend and she could get the address.

The Phoenix officer said Melanie gave a complete description of the suspect Sinsoho including graphic details of tattoos on his arms.

The deputy then spoke with "Anna" who is a social worker at the hospital. Anna said the victim Melanie told her that she was raped by Sinsoho because he believed she had stolen drugs from him. She told the social worker that Sinsoho beat and raped her "for payment" of the stolen drugs. Apparently, he took Melanie into a back room of the house to "talk" about the missing drugs. When they got in the room, Sinsoho locked the door so she couldn't leave. He then slapped her several times and knocked her onto a bed. He then forcibly removed her clothing and raped the 16 year-old girl.

The victim's brother "Joe" was also at the hospital with his sister. Joe told the sheriff's deputy that Melanie arrived at his house around 2:00 a.m. that morning. She told him she had been raped and beaten by a guy she knew as Sun Sinsoho. Joe immediately called the Phoenix Police Department and an officer soon arrived at his house.

When the Phoenix officer saw the victim he had the Phoenix Fire Department paramedics respond to evaluate Melanie's condition. The paramedics determined that

Melanie needed further medical attention and transported her by ambulance to the hospital.

Joe told the sheriff's deputy that his sister was a reported runaway and she had run away from home in the past. He said Melanie is only 16 years old but is already mixed up with the "wrong crowd" and they use drugs. Their family has tried to get Melanie help in the past.

The deputy asked Joe about the clothing Melanie was wearing when she showed up at his house. Joe said he had "bagged" the clothing to give to the police for evidence, but he left the bag at home. Joe drove home and retrieved the bag containing Melanie's clothing and gave it to the deputy.

The deputy notified an on-duty El Mirage Police sergeant about the incident. The sergeant called the Maricopa County Sheriff's Office Special Victims Unit and asked them to respond to the hospital to take over the investigation. Two detectives arrived at the hospital a short time later to interview Melanie.

Prior to the detective's arrival the deputy spoke to Melanie about the incident. She told him more detailed information about the location of the house in El Mirage where she was raped. The deputy also noted that Melanie displayed many of the physical characteristics of a person who uses meth. He documented this information in his report.

When the detectives arrived the deputy briefed them on what he knew of the incident. The deputy ran a "records *check" on Melanie and confirmed that she was a reported "Runaway Juvenile." The detectives told the deputy they would handle the "runaway" issue after they interviewed Melanie.*

The deputy turned over the bag containing the victim's clothing to the Special Victims Unit detectives who were at the hospital and left. He completed his initial report of the incident and turned it to a supervisor for review. The case was now in the hands of the Special Victims Unit.

Findings of the El Mirage Police Review

This was a case that should have been handled immediately by a detective. A forensics "rape kit" should have been completed to collect evidence from the victim. The detectives should have contacted Melanie's friend to get the exact location where the assault occurred in El Mirage. They should have tracked down the known suspect and picked him up for questioning. Apparently, none of this was done.

There are other peripheral issues with the case aside from the fact that the victim was an underage girl and was sexually assaulted. There was significant evidence of drug use by the 30 year-old suspect. With the proper investigative strategy the detectives could have easily secured a search warrant for the home in El Mirage. A proper search warrant affidavit would have given the investigators the lawful right to search the house for evidence of the sexual assault as well as illegal drugs.

Although this case called for further investigation it appears the investigation was never completed by the Special Victims Unit.

Runaway Juveniles

More than 2 million children are reported as runaways each year. In most cases the parents actually know where their child is but the child simply refuses to come home. But, one-third of all runaway cases involve children whose parents do not know their whereabouts. The information in this section provides parents and counselors with background information about the problems associated with runaway juveniles – especially young girls.

Some studies suggest that only about 20% of all runaway juvenile incidents are reported to the police. In most of cases, the parents know where their children are staying and feel it is a "family issue" and no need for police intervention.

The majority of children who run away from home are 15 to 17 years old. Only about 25% of all runaways are age 14 years or younger. Studies show there is no disparity between the number of boys and the number of girls who run away from home each year. Children run away from homes of every socio-economic level, however the majority are from working-class and lower-income homes.

But, studies from the Department of Justice (DOJ), the International Association of Chiefs of Police (IACP) and the Police Executive Research Forum (PERF) all conclude *any* juvenile who runs away from home is more vulnerable to harm than children who remain in their homes under responsible parental supervision.

Statistically, 13 to 16 year-old runaway girls are the most vulnerable. They simply lack the maturity to make good life decisions. It's not long before these girls realize they can't survive on their own and they turn to people whom they believe can be "trusted."

And all too often these are the very people who mean them the most harm. They are typically adult men who prey on young runaway girls. They have no intention of helping these girls and usually exploit, assault or violently victimize them.

Criminal activity among runaway juveniles is at an all-time high. They often start breaking into homes looking for money, food, drugs and alcohol. Some feel they *have* to do these things to survive.

Some runaway girls even turn to prostitution when they unsuspectingly connect with a pimp. Still others may start dealing drugs to survive. Many young runaway girls simply fall deeper into high-risk activities because they no longer feel they have any future.

Runaway vs. Missing

The term "runaway" generally means a child who *intentionally* leaves home (or doesn't return home) without permission.

Most law enforcement agencies classify "runaway juveniles" as a "Missing Person" although the connotations may not be the same. A tag of "runaway" following the "Missing Person" classification does not normally prompt the same response protocol from law enforcement as a true *missing* person.

A child classified as a "Missing Person" (non-runaway) is usually absent from home but not necessarily on their own accord. These are typically children who have been abducted or are young children who may have wandered away from their home and are lost. The police response to these circumstances is much more immediate, specific and manpower-intensive. These situations will generally dictate door-to-door searches, news broadcasts and possibly even an *Amber Alert*.

(According to the United States Department of Justice the AMBER Alert Program is a voluntary partnership between law-enforcement agencies, broadcasters, transportation agencies, and the wireless industry, to activate an urgent bulletin in the most serious child-abduction cases. The goal of an AMBER Alert is to instantly galvanize the entire community to assist in the search for and the safe recovery of an abducted child.)

Police officers and deputies typically handle a Runaway Juvenile call with far less urgency than a true missing or abducted child as described above. Officers normally complete a routine Runaway Juvenile report when the criteria for their specific department policy is met (missing 24 hrs., non-life threatening circumstances, etc.)

In the police report the officer will include all pertinent information about the child and his parents or guardian. The officer will then enter the runaway juvenile's information into the nationwide police computer database National Crime Information Center (NCIC).

If any police officer later has contact with the runaway juvenile, a routine "records check" of the juvenile will show an NCIC "status" of "Missing Person." The officer can then detain the child and notify the parents.

The parents of some runaway juveniles do not easily accept a police department's policy on handling Runaway Juveniles as described above. They often feel a larger police response is warranted to locate their runaway child. This is usually the case when their child has run away from home for the first time.

But, the fact is most juveniles who run away from home generally return home on their own within 24 hrs. Some police agencies even have a 24-hour waiting period before they will actually write a "Runaway Juvenile" report. While there are clear dangers for children who run away from home, most of them do not end up "on the street."

The police will normally examine the "totality of the circumstances" when deciding the type and level of response to a report of a runaway juvenile. The age of the child, their need for medication, their mental capacity and history of prior runaways are all taken into consideration.

The Runaway's Environment

Officers encounter runaway juveniles in many different environments. Runaways tend to congregate with other runaways or with other high-risk groups such as drug and alcohol users.

While investigating crimes, police officers often contact runaways as both victims and offenders. It is not uncommon for officers to encounter runaway juveniles during investigations of prostitution, shoplifting, panhandling, curfew violations and drug/alcohol offenses.

Thankfully, most runaway juveniles are not found by the police as "homeless" or living on the street. The majority of runaways stay with a friend or relative. Nearly 75% of them return home within 24 hrs.

But, this doesn't necessarily eliminate the dangers for runaway juveniles. Some end up staying in an environment with little or no proper adult supervision. This often results in the child becoming involved in criminal behavior or being victimized themselves.

Most runaways occur "spontaneously" during a heated argument or physical conflict. This type of departure is usually unplanned and impulsive. They normally do not bring provisions such as food, clothing or money.

Still others take the time to calculate and plan their departure. They bring clothes, food, money and their personal keepsakes. A runaway juvenile may walk, steal the family car, plan ahead for a ride with friends, use public transportation or even hitchhike. Regardless of how they leave, each of these methods poses their own set of risks to the unsupervised child.

El Mirage Police Report

CASE #06-1050821
Sexual Misconduct With a Minor
Date: March 1, 2006
Victim: 15 year-old female
Suspect: 23 year-old male

This case involves a young girl who had just turned 15 years old and was five months pregnant. Her mother reported her missing and told the police her daughter was in need of medication. The mother believed the girl was in the company of the 23 year-old man who had gotten her pregnant.

Here is the police report:

Facts of the Case:

On March 1, 2006 a uniformed El Mirage police officer was dispatched to a home near 122nd Ave. & Cactus Rd. in El Mirage, Arizona in reference to a runaway 15 year-old girl.

The officer contacted the missing girl's mother "Jan" who said that her daughter "Hope" had been missing for 6 days. She said Hope is an habitual runaway and she last saw her at home on the morning of February 26th when she left for work.

Jan told the officer that her daughter had just turned 15 years old and is five months pregnant. She said Hope may be with the 23 year-old man named "Randy" who got her pregnant. She told the officer that Randy lives in El Mirage and gave him two possible addresses where he might be staying.

The officer asked Jan why her daughter ran away. She told him it was because Hope had wanted to spend the night at Randy's sister's house and she told her "no."

Jan told the officer that last time Hope ran away from home she was missing for nearly six months. She said that Hope is on medication and she was worried about her and the unborn child.

The officer wanted to know why Jan hadn't reported her daughter's pregnancy to the police sooner. She said she spoke to an officer about it but she didn't know Randy's last name at the time. Jan claims that the officer told her *she needed to get the last name before she could make a police report.*

Jan said that she wanted charges brought against Randy for Sexual Misconduct with her underage daughter.

The officer then completed a Missing Persons report on Hope and entered the information into N.C.I.C. (National Crime Information Center) and A.C.I.C. (Arizona Crime Information Center) law enforcement databases along with a photograph of Hope.

The case was assigned to a Maricopa County Sheriff detective on April 5, 2006 and was reassigned to the Special Victims Unit on April 25, 2006.

Findings of the El Mirage Police Review

There was a clear indication this runaway girl was likely in the company of a 23 year-old man. The investigators should have made a concerted effort to locate both the victim and the suspect in this case. The girl had just turned 15 years-old and had gotten pregnant when she was only 14 years-old. If the identified 23 year-old man was in fact the father of the unborn child he should have been charged with Sexual Misconduct With a Minor or Statutory Rape.

While the sexual activity may have been consensual on her part, this 15 year-old girl was still the victim of sexual misconduct. She was now pregnant, missing and in need of medication. This case clearly warranted immediate follow up investigation by detectives.

Records indicate this case was assigned to a Special Victims Unit detective in April 2006. However, based on the information in the report it appears that nothing more was done with this investigation.

Why Children Run Away

Children run away from homes and foster care facilities every day for a variety of different reasons. The vast majority of runaways choose to leave on their own. However, in some situations their parents actually *tell* them to leave.

In discussions with parents many believed their child ran away because the child was "rebellious" against the parent. But studies have shown that most children who run away are victims of dysfunctional or abusive families or foster homes.

Children tend to run away from families that are unwilling or unable to work through problems in the home. Poor communication between parents and children is a prime reason that children run away from home. Children tend to run away when the conflict in the home escalates to a point where they feel the situation is hopeless. They often feel the only option is to leave.

But, the inability of parents and children to communicate over "parenting" issues isn't the only reason children run away from home. Some are trying to get away from very serious situations.

Physical or sexual abuse by family members or step-parents and drug/alcohol abuse in the home are sometimes the cause of children running away. Other reasons include rejection due to sexual orientation, pregnancy, failing grades and domestic violence.

Regardless of the reason a child runs away from home, the dangers they face in an environment without responsible adult supervision are always the same.

Most veteran police officers know that run away juveniles often display signs of physical and sexual abuse, alcohol and drug problems, depression and other social issues.

Runaway Juveniles A Complex Issue

Law enforcement faces many different issues pertaining to runaway juveniles. The reasons children run away are a complex and a deep-rooted social issue.

Most police agencies cannot effectively impact the *causes* behind the issue of runaway juveniles. They simply concentrate on ways to reduce the dangers *to* the runaway juveniles, and the crimes committed *by* them when they run away from home.

Being a "Runaway Juvenile" is considered a "status offense" (a non-crime) and limits the options available to police officers. When they contact a reported runaway juvenile the officer has the legal right to detain the child and return them to their parent or guardian. But, most juvenile detention facilities will not hold a runaway juvenile simply because the child is incorrigible or the parents are uncooperative.

Runaway juveniles often suffer medical issues from poor nutrition, poor hygiene, and exposure to the elements. And due to their high-risk lifestyle runaways are also susceptible to sexually transmitted diseases. Their unhealthy and stressful lifestyle also makes them prone to depression, suicide and other mental disorders.

Discovering a child has run away from home can be a very emotional event for a parent. A parent's emotions over a runaway child typically run the gambit between worry, self-blame, guilt, remorse and anger.

Some parents phase into a "denial" mode and convince themselves their child is merely staying with a friend. But, most parents try to find the juvenile by calling their friends and relatives. And some will call the police to report the missing child.

Most runaway juveniles don't venture too far from their homes. Only about one-fourth of all runaways ever leave the general vicinity of their homes. An even fewer number leave the state in which they are living.

Very few runaways ever consider the dangers they face by leaving home. Most of them believe they will stay safely with a friend or relative. Due to their young age and lack of maturity most runaways do not grasp the risks they face of falling victim to predatory adults, drugs and violent crime.

The longer a child is away from the supervision of their responsible parents, the more likely they are to being victimized. Formerly "accommodating" friends or relatives may tire of them and force them to leave. The runaway may then face other dangers associated with self-survival.

A runaway's need for food, shelter and money may drive them into high-risk activities such as theft, substance use, consensual sex with adults, and even prostitution. Some runaway girls fall prey to predatory adults.

Nearly all runaway juveniles eventually return to their homes. Most of them return on their own while others are located by a parent, relative or the police. Many return with the hope that things will be better at home and they can reconcile their differences. Many return simply because they are disenchanted or tired of the difficult lifestyle of a runaway.

Runaway Prevention

Understanding the reasons children run away from home is an important step for parents. Recognizing and addressing the issues with their children can help prevent a child from making the "life-changing" decision to run away from home. Very seldom does any "good" occur when a child runs away from home.

It is important that parents effectively communicate with their children. Parents need to *listen* to what their children have to say. A child needs to know they can confide in their parent or guardian if they are abused or exploited in their home.

Starting at an early age parents should spend time with their children. Parents should explain the real dangers of running away from home and build a foundation of trust with their child.

Young people today are bombarded with influences outside the home. Through the Internet, movies, electronic media and their peers, young people today are exposed to more outside influences than any previous generation.

But, studies have shown that parents *do matter* in the lives of their children. Children need the support, guidance, and caring that parents provide within the home. Older children often comment they *want* to hear from their parents about issues or concerns.

Child experts collectively recommend that effective parenting includes acknowledging your child's appropriate behavior; being a good role model; being consistent with rules and discipline; admitting your own mistakes; using open dialogue with your children; and, being a good listener by providing the child with your undivided attention.

Parenting is clearly one of life's most challenging responsibilities. Children learn through the examples of their parents. They depend on their parents to develop proper life skills, good judgment and responsible decision-making.

Parents who practice these skills will develop a better relationship with their children and may prevent them from ever running away from home.

****

Chapter 9

Child Molesters and Pedophiles

Chapter 9 examines the details of five police reports that were mishandled by the Maricopa County Sheriff's Office. The victims of these crimes were all young girls who were sexually molested by adult males. The youngest victim was a 2 year-old girl and the oldest was 13 years old.

This chapter also includes important information about child molesters and pedophiles. It describes their psychological profile and how they stalk young children. Also included in this chapter is information and guidance for parents on ways to protect their children from sexual predators.

El Mirage Police Report

CASE # 07-11221010
Child Molesting
April 4, 2007
Victim: 6 year-old female
Suspect: 38 year-old male

This case involves a 6 year-old girl who was at home playing in her room. Her father was outside working on his vehicle when the girl's 38 year-old uncle stopped by for a visit. The uncle came in the house and touched the little girl inappropriately. A Maricopa County Sheriff's deputy was called to investigate.

Here is the police report:

Facts of the Case:

On April 4, 2007 around 4:00 a.m. a Maricopa County Sheriff's deputy was dispatched to a Phoenix area hospital. He was responding on a radio call of a possible Child Molesting that occurred at a home in the city of El Mirage. The Maricopa County Sheriff's Office was under contract to provide police service to El Mirage so a sheriff's deputy was summoned to do the investigation.

When the deputy arrived at the hospital he contacted "Phillip" who said he had called the police about his 6 year-old daughter "Melissa." Phillip said that yesterday evening around 5:00 p.m. he was out in front of his house on North Main Street in El Mirage working on his car when his uncle "Thomas" came over to visit. Phillip said he continued to work on his car and Thomas went inside the house.

About an hour later Phillip went in the house and found his 6 year-old daughter Melissa lying on the living room floor with Thomas "laying or hovering over her" on his hands and knees. When Thomas saw Phillip he quickly tried to get off Melissa and immediately walked into another room.

Phillip said they both had their clothes on but it looked totally inappropriate. He said he was very concerned about what he had just seen. He asked Melissa what was going on and she said Thomas wanted to play a "tickling game." Phillip said he asked his daughter some specific questions about what Thomas had done to her. The young girl said that Thomas was "moving his body in a specific way on top of her" but she couldn't really describe it to her father.

Phillip said he then went in the other room and confronted Thomas about what he had been doing with Melissa. Thomas said he was just playing a "tickling game" with her. Phillip wasn't satisfied with that answer but he knew Thomas wasn't going to say anything more.

A short while later Phillip's sister "Charlene" came over to the house. He told her what he had seen and asked her to talk to Melissa. Charlene talked to the little girl about what had happened and she told Charlene the same basic story but did add "a few more details." Charlene did not share those details with Phillip but suggested they take Melissa to the hospital emergency room to have her checked out.

The deputy said he spoke to the doctor who examined Melissa. The doctor said he conducted an external examination of Melissa's genital area and found no signs of trauma, no tenderness at the entrance of the vagina, and trace amounts of a white discharge which he explained is common for young children.

The nurse who assisted with the examination said she asked Melissa if her uncle Thomas had taken off her clothes while playing the "tickling game" and she said "yes." The nurse asked the girl if he ever touched her "pee-pee" and the little girl replied "no."

The deputy then notified a supervisor of the situation and he notified the Special Victims Unit. A short while later the deputy was notified that the detectives wanted to interview the child and to have her father transport her to a nearby sheriff's facility.

Phillip said he would bring his daughter to the sheriff's office as soon as she was discharged from the hospital.

The deputy then notified Child Protective Services about the situation. He completed his report and turned it in to his supervisor.

Findings of the El Mirage Police Review

The information provided in the deputy's initial report indicates the case was turned over to the Special Victims Unit and they were going to interview the child and take over the investigation.

However, a review of this report revealed nothing beyond the responding deputy's initial report. The El Mirage Police Department requested a complete copy of the Maricopa County Sheriff's Office investigation to see if the Special Victims Unit ever concluded this case.

El Mirage was told the case had been "closed" and "Exceptionally Cleared" by the Special Victims Unit. There was no documentation or explanation in the report as to how they arrived at that conclusion. Nothing in the report shows the investigation was ever completed.

"STRANGER DANGER"

Most people picture the typical child molester as a dirty old man in a trench coat trying to lure children into his car. They don't consider a family friend, relative or neighbor. They don't imagine their child's coach, teacher or playmate's family member.

Occasionally, the overt and blatant child abduction by a stranger still occurs but those instances are rare. "Stranger Danger" and other awareness campaigns have been effective in training our children to be wary and avoid contact with strangers.

The more common molesters are people who are known to the child and have gained the child's trust or confidence. They often seduce children through intimidation, persuasion and fear.

The most dangerous phenomenon of child molesters, predators and pedophiles is their *lifelong* propensity for deviant sexual behavior with children. Their sexual attraction to children is not a learned behavior that can be rehabilitated through incarceration or counseling. Child molesters nearly always re-offend if given the opportunity.

The Child Molester Psyche

Children are naturally vulnerable to adults. In our society adults extend power and influence over children. Child molesters exploit their authority over children

and manipulate it for their personal benefit. Therefore, most any child can be at risk.

Pedophiles have distinct characteristics and prefer children of a certain age. By definition pedophiles are "obsessed" with children and often display other "obsessive-compulsive" tendencies.

Many pedophiles spend their entire life planning different schemes to get close to children. The life of a pedophile is driven by the sexual fantasies they create about children.

Child molesters and pedophiles carefully select and scrutinize their potential victims. Parents should be aware that adult male child predators often target girls who are too young to get pregnant.

Most studies generally agree that many child molesters have a history of mistreatment themselves. Many had been sexually or physically abused – or both.

Child molesters are rarely found to have any empathy for the children they victimize. Even though they may have been a child-victim themselves, they often have difficulty perceiving the consequences of their actions from their victim's perspective.

Understanding the psyche of child molesters and pedophiles is an important element of awareness. Most of them know that sexually abusing children is wrong. However, many will justify their actions by convincing themselves that it is somehow the "child's fault." Some will "legitimize" their actions by telling themselves that the child "enjoyed" the sexual contact.

Psychologists who study the behaviors of child molesters conclude that many are socially awkward. They often have issues with intimacy with partners their own age. They typically display poor interpersonal and communication skills among adults – especially in a personal relationship.

El Mirage Police Report

CASE # 06-1050819
Sexual Misconduct With a Minor
July 7, 2006
Victim: 13 year-old female
Suspect: 18 year-old male

This case involves an 18 year-old man who befriended a 13 year-old girl against the wishes of her parents. The girl's parents found out the man had taken advantage of their daughter by allowing her to drink alcohol and then engaging in inappropriate sexual conduct with her. They called the police.

Here is the police report:

Facts of the Case:

On July 7, 2006 an El Mirage police officer was dispatched to the visitor's lobby at the police station to meet a man concerning a sexual misconduct case. The officer contacted "Edward" who told him that he found out that an 18 year-old man had sexual contact with his 13 year-old daughter "Brittany."

Edward went on to tell the officer that he learned this information from his live-in girlfriend "Sharon." He told the officer that Brittany and her girlfriend went to visit a group of other friends in El Mirage a few days earlier. Edward said that he found out that the girls had been drinking and that Brittany had sexual contact with an 18 year-old man named "Josh."

The officer asked Edward what type of sexual contact he was referring to and he told the officer she had "masturbated Josh's penis." The officer asked Edward if Brittany was forced into doing it and he said "no." As far as he knew it was consensual but he was concerned that an adult man had taken advantage of his 13 year-old daughter.

Edward told the officer that Brittany has known Josh for a while. She first met him when she used to live in El Mirage with her mother. He said that both he and Brittany's mother did not want Brittany hanging around with Josh but she wouldn't listen.

The officer asked Edward if he had personally spoken to Brittany about the incident. Edward said he had not spoken to Brittany but had gotten all the information from his girlfriend Sharon.

Edward provided the officer with Josh's full name, address, and phone number to help locate him for this investigation.

The officer then interviewed Edward's live-in girlfriend Sharon who said she found out about the incident from her own 14 year-old daughter "Debbie." Brittany had apparently confided in Debbie and told her that she and Josh had been drinking at the get-together in El Mirage on July 3, 2006.

Brittany told Debbie that she and Josh started kissing and one thing led to another and that she gave Josh a "hand job." According to Debbie, Brittany and Josh did not have sexual intercourse.

The officer concluded his interview with Sharon. Debbie was not available so the officer did not interview her.

Edward told the officer that he was going to file an injunction to keep Josh away from his minor daughter. He also said that he would assist in prosecuting Josh.

The El Mirage patrol officer did a thorough job of gathering and documenting details about this crime. However, the information he received was all second-hand and needed to be validated.

Brittany (victim) and Debbie (witness) both needed to be interviewed. And certainly Josh needed to be picked up for questioning. The officer was aware that this follow up work would be done by detectives.

The officer completed his report and turned it in to his sergeant. The case was sent to the Maricopa County Sheriff's Office Special Victims Unit for further investigation and follow up.

A supplemental report by a sergeant indicates the case was sent to the detectives of the Special Victims Unit on July 19, 2006.

Findings of the El Mirage Police Review

This was another case that clearly warranted further investigation by detectives. Most importantly, the identity of the suspect was known and he should have been picked up and interviewed about the allegations.

According to the report, the Maricopa County Sheriff's Office Special Victims Unit was notified of this incident on July 19, 2006. However, it appears that the sheriff's office did not complete this case and it was returned to El Mirage in 2007. The sheriff's report indicates this case was "Exceptionally Cleared."

There is no information in the Maricopa County Sheriff's report that explains why this case was "Exceptionally Cleared" and not investigated by their Special Victims Unit.

Common Traits Of Child Molesters

Researchers, police officers and treatment providers who routinely deal with these individuals agree on certain traits and patterns among molesters.

This is *not* meant to imply that all individuals who display these characteristics are child molesters. It is simply a group of indicators that parents should consider among the "totality of circumstances" in protecting their children.

Clearly, not all child molesters or potential molesters exhibit *all* of these behaviors or patterns - some are *very* difficult to detect. When the crimes of a child molester are revealed, friends and family members often express shock or disbelief that the person is a child molester.

Statistically, most child predators and molesters are adult males, although women are also known to molest young boys and girls. There is no known socio-economic difference in child molesters. They come from all walks of life with no differentiation in race, religion or employment.

The majority of adult child molesters are not exclusively attracted to children. Many are married and most have relationships with other adults. However, adult male child molesters who are married often describe their marriage as a "companionship" rather than a marriage. They often have little or no sexual contact with their spouse.

Only a small percentage of pedophiles have an exclusive attraction to children. However, they are the *most* dangerous because their entire emotional and sexual focus is with children. They typically have no interest in adult partners, usually remain unmarried and maintain a lifelong interest in children.

These individuals usually relate better to children and feel more comfortable with child-level interests. Child molesters usually display an interest in children within a specific age group and only one gender.

Child molesters and predators sometimes are employed or volunteer with youth programs and organized athletics. Some become scout leaders, child-care providers and employees of businesses that cater to young children (arcades, playgrounds, child-oriented pizza parlors, etc.) Others seek out children from troubled or lower income homes.

Another trademark of pedophiles is their desire to develop a positive reputation within their community. They strive to convince parents and other adults that they are trustworthy. Part of their strategy is to create an image in which parents feel comfortable allowing them around their children.

Again, it is important to reiterate that many people posses one or more of the behavior characteristics explained in this chapter but are *not* child molesters. Similarly, some child molesters may not display *any* of these traits and will be difficult to detect. This information simply describes common traits compiled from years of research into the behavior of child molesters and pedophiles.

El Mirage Police Report

CASE # 06-1050814
Sexual Misconduct With a Minor
December 23, 2006
Victim: 12-year old female
Suspect: 26-year old male

This case involves a 12 year-old girl who started displaying emotional and behavioral problems at home. When the family addressed the girl's issues she disclosed that her 26-year old cousin had coaxed her into having sex with him and she was now pregnant. The cousin had threatened to hurt her family if she told anyone she had sex with him. The parents called the police.

Here is the police report:

Facts of the Case:

On December 23, 2006 an El Mirage police officer responded to a home in the 13800 block of N. Primrose Street in reference to a 911 call of an "Unknown Trouble." When the officer arrived he saw several people in the front yard of the home. He also saw a young girl crying and being comforted by another male and female. The officer made contact with a woman who identified herself as "Florica." The officer had trouble communicating with Florica because she only spoke Spanish.

However, through his limited Spanish the officer was able to determine that she had just learned that her 12-year old daughter "Juliana" had gotten pregnant by her 26-year old cousin. The officer determined that Juliana was the young girl who was crying in the yard and being comforted by other family members.

The officer recognized the seriousness of this situation and asked Florica to come to the El Mirage Police station where she could be interviewed by a Spanish-speaking officer. About an hour later the El Mirage officer, with the assistance of a translator began an in-depth interview of Florica at the police station.

As the interview began Florica told the officer that she noticed something was wrong with her 12-year old daughter Juliana and asked her what was bothering her. Juliana said she was having problems at school with another girl. Florica said she did not believe that was all that was bothering her daughter and she kept pressing her for more information.

Florica said she eventually asked her daughter if she was pregnant. She said that Juliana started to cry and admitted that she was pregnant. Florica asked Juliana who had gotten her pregnant but she wouldn't answer her mother. Juliana was apparently very emotional about the whole situation but eventually told her mother that she had sex with her 26-year old cousin "Vincent."

Florica said that Juliana told her that Vincent said he would do something to hurt her family if she told anyone he had sex with her. Juliana told her mother she was afraid to say anything fearing what Vincent might do to her family.

As the interview continued Florica told the officer she was aware that Vincent had also gotten another 14-year old relative pregnant. Florica provided the officer with specific information about Vincent and where he stays. She also told the officer that she believed Vincent was currently in Tennessee working. She said he comes and goes between Arizona and Tennessee and he would eventually return to Arizona.

The officer explained to Florica that detectives would take over the case and arrange for a forensic interview of Juliana. He told her that it would be best if no one discussed the details of the incident with Juliana until the forensic interview was done. The officer also told Florica that it is best that no one contacts Vincent until the detectives talk to him.

The officer completed his initial report and it was sent to the Maricopa County Sheriff's Office Special Victims Unit for follow up investigation.

Findings of the El Mirage Police Review

For obvious reasons this was a serious case that required follow up by detectives. The 26-year old suspect had sex with his 12-year old cousin and threatened her family if she told anyone. There was also information that he had sex with another minor-aged relative. If these allegations were true this suspect had all the signs of a child predator.

According to the report, the Maricopa County Sheriff's Office Special Victims Unit was initially assigned this case for follow up investigation in December 2006. However, a review of the case by the El Mirage Police Department showed no further investigation was ever completed.

Effective Manipulators

A child predator often prefers child-oriented activities rather than normal adult activities. They often engage in hobbies that would likely attract young children. Their home or favorite room within the home may be decorated with "child-oriented' wall paper, furniture and popular toys.

As depicted in several of the police reports in this book a child molester may use a variety of techniques or tricks to gain the friendship, confidence and trust of their victim.

They will often use fear, bribery, promises or even physical force to get close to their victims.

However, it is not uncommon for a child to become emotionally attached to their molester as they are being systematically victimized. They may even develop a desire to please him or gain his approval. Over time, the child may have difficulty distinguishing between appropriate and inappropriate behavior with their abuser.

Many child molesters initially conceal their true intent of pursuing a child for sexual purposes. They often attempt to form an emotional bond with the child by privately sharing their own personal feelings of loneliness with the child.

It may take weeks or months but the molester's goal is to gain the child's sympathy. They manipulate the child's sympathy into physical affection which eventually leads to sexual contact. This is often the case where young girls are molested by their mother's live-in boyfriend or step-father.

Child molesters become masters of manipulation. They work hard to build the child's self-esteem and make the child believe they are special.

Pedophiles are also attentive listeners. They listen and learn about a child's likes and dislikes, and then exploit that information to their own benefit.

Unfortunately, shy and withdrawn children are often the target of child predators. The pedophile may begin the seduction with much needed attention or gifts. They will often promise the child trips to fun places such as the zoo, the movies or an amusement park.

Child molesters frequently offer to babysit, provide care or take children on trips to further manipulate their victim. It is not uncommon for adult child-predators to involve their victims in activities that the child's parents would *never* allow.

Pedophiles and child molesters will often lure a child with adult activities such as drinking alcohol or watching sexually explicit movies. They often convince a child they are "mature for their age" and allow them to participate in these activities because they are so "mature." In reality they are simply manipulating the child's emotions for their own benefit.

It is not uncommon for a child molester to blackmail or bribe their victim after the fact. By threatening to expose the child's sexual behavior with them, a molester may intimidate the child into extending the relationship. Through fear, embarrassment or shame a child victim is often coerced into hiding or continuing the inappropriate sexual conduct.

El Mirage Police Report

CASE # 07-1050839
Sexual Misconduct With a Minor
Date: August 19, 2007
Victim: 8 year-old female
Suspect: 38 year-old male (approximately)

This case involves a 15 year-old girl had been molested by her step-father since she was 8 years old. She was routinely made to go on trips alone with her step-father and the molesting occurred while they were away. The girl disclosed the sexual misconduct to her boyfriend who notified the police.

Here is the police report:

Facts of the Case:

On August 19, 2007 around 6:30 p.m. a Maricopa County Sheriff's deputy received a message from his dispatcher to contact a man named "James." The dispatcher told him that James wanted to report that his girlfriend "Crystal" had been the victim of molesting by her step-father for the past eight years. The Maricopa County Sheriff's Office was under contract to provide police service to El Mirage so a sheriff's deputy was summoned to do the investigation.

The deputy called James to get the details of what had occurred. James explained that his girlfriend Crystal disclosed to him that she had been the victim of child molesting by her step-father "Alton" for the past eight *years. James said that Crystal is now 16 years old and the molesting started when she was 8 years old.*

James told the deputy that Crystal first reported Alton molesting her when she was 8 years old. The allegation was investigated by the police but later dropped. Crystal told James she had been pressured by her family back then to drop the charges. She said they made her feel guilty and told her she would be the "reason Alton went to jail."

Apparently, Alton's job required him to travel by car around the state of Arizona and many times he took Crystal with him on the trips. The last time Crystal reported going on such a trip with Alton was April 20, 2007.

Crystal said on that trip Alton put his hand inside her pants and inserted his finger into her vagina. Then he told her to touch his penis and she "did as she was told to do." Crystal said she didn't tell anyone – including her parents about this incident.

James told the deputy that he believed that Crystal's mother "Rita" has been aware of what Alton was doing to her daughter for quite a while. He said she played down the seriousness of it because she did not want to "lose the financial security" Alton was providing to the family.

James told the deputy that Rita recently told him that she thought it was "bullshit" that her husband Alton would rather touch her 15-year old daughter than touch her.

That's when James was convinced that Rita knew what Alton was doing to Crystal.

Crystal's mother had recently confided in James that she was planning to leave Alton. She was planning to relocate out of state and not let Alton know where she was. Rita said she was tired of Alton's constant threatening and intimidating. She told James that Alton once put a gun to her head and threatened her.

The deputy asked James how often Crystal had gone with Alton on these trips. He told the deputy it was every 1-3 months over the past several years. James also said that Alton only touches Crystal when they are on the road and never does it at home.

The deputy asked if he knew whether Alton ever had sexual intercourse with Crystal. James said Crystal has never mentioned that so he assumed it has not occurred. But, he did not know that for sure.

James said that Crystal now refuses to go on the trips with Alton. The family routinely makes excuses for Crystal in order to prevent her from going with Alton.

The deputy gathered the necessary information he needed to file his report including the names, address and personal information on all the parties involved. He then wrote his initial report on the incident and turned it in to his supervisor.

According to the report the sergeant notified the sergeant of the Maricopa County Sheriff's Office Special Victims

Unit and the case was referred to her for follow up and disposition. The deputy's original report also was forwarded to the Special Victims Unit.

Findings of the El Mirage Police Review

This case appeared to have some very serious allegations. If true, this girl had been victimized over many years since she was 8 years old and was still living in the same household with the offender. Clearly, this case warranted follow up investigation by the detectives.

It also appears that jurisdiction may be an issue with this case. The investigators would have to establish the locations where the molesting took place. That could be done most effectively through a forensic interview of the victim. The detectives should have arranged for an interview at the Child Help facility in Phoenix or Southwest Family Advocacy Center in Goodyear or Glendale.

A review of the report indicates that the Special Victims Unit was notified of the case but it appears this investigation was never completed.

In early 2008 an El Mirage detective contacted a sheriff's sergeant and told him the case appeared incomplete. The sheriff's sergeant told the El Mirage detective that the case had been "Exceptionally Cleared" but could not explain why they closed the case.

How They Get Caught

Operating in secrecy is the key to success for a child molester or pedophile. Their actions are typically well-planned and meticulously calculated to avoid detection. They carefully select their target and expend whatever time is necessary to manipulate and exploit the young victim.

The child crimes of a clever pedophile can go undetected for decades. Many victims do not disclose what happened to them for many years.

Some child molesters or pedophiles will get caught because they become careless – although not very often. Others will be discovered when a wary parent sees "indicators" that something is physically or emotionally wrong with their child. Some molesters get "caught in the act" when a parent, friend or family member simply shows up unexpectedly.

In later years, many child victims suffer severe emotional issues and are unable to sustain a healthy relationship. They will often disclose their experiences during a counseling session which can prompt a police investigation. Still others simply grow up and disclose what happened to them. They are often motivated to protect other children from similar consequences.

However, some children *do* report being victimized in a timelier manner. A child might complain of pain or a parent may discover physical signs of sexual abuse and seek medical examination for their child.

Other children begin to display serious emotional or behavioral patterns that could suggest sexual abuse. In those cases, parents should seek professional counseling or therapy to determine the cause of the emotional changes in their child.

Children living with their parents or guardian in an open and trusting environment are most likely to reveal if they have been the victim of a child molester.

Many law enforcement officers will agree that when a child molester or pedophile is caught it is typically not their first offense. Follow up investigations often reveal previously undetected victims of child-crimes, child pornography and evidence of other sexual deviancy.

As mentioned above, experienced police investigators know that pedophiles often possess and covet child pornography. Search warrants of the homes of child molesters typically reveal computers filled with images of child porn, CD's and videos of child porn and other child erotica.

El Mirage Police Report

CASE # 07-1122109
Child Molesting
July 22, 2007
Victim: 2 year-old female
Suspect: Adult male

This case involves a 2 year-old girl who was routinely left in the care of female "housemates" while her mother was at work. The child began displaying odd behavior and emotional outbursts around her family. They also noticed some suspicious marks in her genitals area and brought the little girl in for an examination. The evidence suggested the child had been molested.

An adult male also shared the house with the mother and her children. The mother found out the male had a long history of molesting children. The authorities were notified and a Maricopa County Sheriff's deputy was dispatched to investigate.

Here is the police report:

Facts of the Case:

On July 22, 2007 around 5:00 p.m. a Maricopa County Sheriff's deputy was dispatched to a hospital in west Phoenix. He was responding on a radio call of a possible Child Molesting that occurred at a home in the city of El Mirage. The Maricopa County Sheriff's Office was under contract to provide police service to El Mirage so a sheriff's deputy was summoned to do the investigation.

When the deputy arrived at the hospital he contacted "Karen" who said she was the one who called the police. Karen told the deputy she was living at a residence in El Mirage in the 11700 block of West Sweetwater Ave. with her daughters "Meagan" (age 2 years) and "Zuri" (age 18 months). They were sharing the residence with another family that included three adults and five other children.

Karen said she worked in the medical field with a rotating schedule and usually worked 6:00 p.m. to 8:00 a.m. She said when she was at work her two daughters were generally cared for by two of the other adult women who lived in the house.

She told the deputy that over the past 4-5 weeks she began seeing some behavioral changes in her 2 year-old daughter Meagan. Karen said she noticed temper tantrums, resistance in going to sleep at night, being "clingy" and isolationism from adults. She recently noticed when she was changing her diaper Meagan didn't want her to touch her private parts complaining that it hurt.

Karen's mother "Diana" was also at the hospital and the deputy spoke with her. Diana said that her granddaughter Meagan spent the night with her about a week ago and she noticed Meagan was acting odd. Diana said she walked in the living room and found Meagan on the couch. She said the little girl had her diaper off and was lying on her back with her legs up in the air rubbing her vaginal area. Diana said she examined her granddaughter and noticed some bruises on her lower legs.

Karen said Meagan was complaining about vaginal pain again today and became concerned that something might have happened to her while being baby sat. She told the deputy she had become concerned that Meagan was being sexually assaulted or molested by one of the adults living at the Sweetwater address. Fearing the worst, Karen brought Meagan into the hospital to be checked out.

Karen told the deputy there were two adult females and one adult male living in the house. She provided the deputy with the names of the two women and said the man's name was "Rick." She described him as an older man but did not know his date of birth.

According to Karen, Rick once confided in her that he had been accused of molesting his own daughters while living in another state. He told her that he had to take classes and participate in "special programs" in order to "clear the charges."

Based on the totality of the circumstances Karen told the deputy she suspects Rick has been molesting her daughter Meagan.

The deputy then spoke with the attending nurse who assisted the doctor that treated Meagan. The nurse said the doctor examined the little girl's vaginal area and found swelling and redness in the area, but no tearing or abrasions. She said they did not conduct a sexual assault examination.

Karen told the deputy she did want the matter investigated and she would assist in prosecution. She signed a medical release form and gave it to the deputy.

The deputy then notified Child Protective Services about the situation. He completed his report and turned it in to his supervisor.

Findings of the El Mirage Police Review

The responding deputy recognized this appeared to be a valid Child Molesting against a 2 year-old girl. This case clearly warranted further investigation by detectives. The information provided in the deputy's initial report provided sufficient leads to begin the investigation. The case should have been forwarded to the Special Victims Unit for follow up investigation. The 2 year-old victim should have been given a forensic interview.

The detectives should have determined whether the suspect was a Registered Sex Offender after being charged with molesting his own children.

However, a review of this report showed no further investigation was ever conducted by the Special Victims Unit. The El Mirage Police Department requested a complete copy of the Maricopa County Sheriff's Office investigation. Based on the report they provided it appears that nothing more was ever done on this investigation.

Protect Your Children

In 1996, the United States congress passed Megan's Law. It was based on the murder of 7 year-old Megan Kanka of Piscataway Township, New Jersey. In 1994 Megan was kidnapped, raped and murdered by a neighbor who was a convicted sex offender.

Megan's Law and subsequent similar state laws authorize law enforcement agencies to inform the public about the existence and identity of a sex-offender living in their neighborhood. The laws were enacted to expose pedophiles and enhance a parent's ability to protect their children.

Nearly every state in the United States has a local "convicted sex offender" database that is available to the public. The Arizona Department of Public Safety oversees the Sex Offender program and website www.azsexoffender.org for the state of Arizona.

The purpose of the Arizona website is to provide information to the public about the location of sex offenders within Arizona. The website works in conjunction with individual police departments throughout the state. It is an educational mechanism to make the public aware of the potential threat that sex offenders pose to the people of Arizona.

Informing the public about the potential threat of sex offenders living in their community is an important first step towards preventing future sexual assaults and child molesting.

Molesters have to operate in an environment of secrecy with their victims. Therefore, the most effective way for parents to protect their children from molesters is through open and continuous communication with them. Parents should educate their children about avoiding high-risk situations and being aware of their surroundings.

Most children need to feel comfortable before they will disclose their true inner feelings with their parents. This is even more difficult for a child who is feeling "uncomfortable" about a situation that involves another adult or family member.

"Human nature" can easily cause a parent to refuse to see the possibility that their child has been molested. Shame, guilt or devotion to their child can send an otherwise responsible parent into "denial" of the fact their child has been molested.

But, parental denial is *extremely* dangerous for their child. It only prolongs the child's suffering and allows the abuser to remain undetected.

It is extremely important that parents remain vigilant to any signs or "indicators" that their children may have been sexually abused. And, it is equally important that parents respond to those indicators in an appropriate and *timely* manner.

Chapter 10

"Live-in" Boyfriends, Step-fathers and House Guests

Chapter 10 includes *five* police reports in which young girls were sexually molested or abused within their "family" environment. In each of these cases, the offender was their mother's live-in boyfriend, their step-father or another person cohabitating with their family. The victims of these crimes were all girls between the ages of 2 and 15 years old. These police reports were among the dozens of investigations mishandled by the Maricopa County Sheriff's Office.

This chapter also includes information about the potential problems children face when cohabitating in a "family" setting. Also included is extensive information for parents about sexual abuse recognition and prevention.

El Mirage Police Report

CASE # 07-1050837
Sexual Misconduct With a Minor
Date: June 14, 2007
Victim: 12 year-old female
Suspect: 35 year-old male

This case involves a woman's live-in boyfriend who exposed himself to her 11 and 12 year-old daughters while alone in their backyard swimming pool. The 12 year-old girl also believed her mom's boyfriend was fondling her at night while she slept. A Maricopa County Sheriff's deputy was called to investigate.

Here is the police report:

Facts of the Case:

On June 14, 2007 about 8:15 p.m. a Maricopa County Sheriff's deputy responded to a home in the 12300 block of W. Flores Drive El Mirage on a Domestic Violence call. The Maricopa County Sheriff's Office was under contract to provide police service to El Mirage so a sheriff's deputy was summoned to handle the call.

While the deputy was enroute to the call the radio dispatcher advised him that the complainant's name was "Anamarie" and she was fighting with her 35 year-old live-in boyfriend "Juan" and wanted Juan out of the house.

Just as the deputy arrived at the scene he saw a man fitting the description of Juan walking out of the house attempting to leave. The deputy described him as being agitated and irate. When the deputy stopped the man and asked his name he said it was "Juan." The deputy temporarily detained him until he could figure out what was going on.

The deputy was alone at the call so he put handcuffs on Juan and placed him the backseat of his patrol car. A records check revealed that Juan had no outstanding warrants but did have a suspended driver's license. The deputy then went in the house to contact Anamarie to find out what happened.

Anamarie told the deputy that the argument with Juan had been verbal only. Anamarie said she called the police earlier that day because Juan was a few hours late coming home from work. She said it was his first day on a new job at Wal-Mart and she was concerned that something happened. When Juan got home later that day an argument started and she told him to leave.

She also told the deputy that earlier in the day her two daughters disclosed to her that Juan had been inappropriately touching her youngest daughter 12 year-old "Anna." The girls also told their mother that Juan had exposed his penis to them while in the swimming pool.

When the deputy heard the allegations of Child Molesting by Anamarie and her daughters he notified his supervisor. The sergeant directed the deputy to contact the sergeant of the Special Victims Unit. The deputy asked the radio dispatcher to page the detective sergeant and ask her to call him.

Apparently, the girls told Anamarie that two days earlier they had been in the backyard pool with Juan when he exposed his penis. They told their mother Juan's penis was erect and they both saw it. The girls said that Juan was "staring at Anna the whole time." Anna and her sister told their mother, "it was sticking out and he had a boner." Anamarie said she apparently was in the house when this occurred.

The deputy asked why the girls didn't report this to her sooner. Anamarie said she asked the same question and the girls told her they were afraid of him. They said he didn't have a job and he was "always around." The girls said after he left they felt comfortable telling their mother.

Anamarie told the deputy that two weeks ago 12 year-old Anna told her that unusual things had been happening to her at night while she slept. She told her mother that she felt someone touching her all over her body. Anna sometimes slept with her sister but the touching only happened when she slept alone. Anna told her mother she believes it was Juan touching her.

The deputy asked why she didn't report that to the police when she first learned about it. Anamarie said she wanted to gather more evidence and have more facts before calling the police.

Anamarie explained to the deputy that when her older daughter Anna was 11 years old she was molested by her *step-father. She called the police and reported it but the charges were dropped due to a "lack of evidence." Her daughter went through a lot over that ordeal and her ex-husband was never prosecuted. This time she wanted to make sure she had enough evidence first.*

Anamarie suspects it was Juan who was touching her daughter while she slept. She said she did want him prosecuted for touching Anna as well as exposing himself to both girls.

The deputy explained that Juan was going to be released at this time pending further investigation. He would not be allowed back in the house and the deputy would help Juan arrange for a place to stay – with a friend or relative. The deputy also told Anamarie how to obtain an Order of Protection against Juan to keep him away from them.

Anamarie was told the case would be turned over to detectives who would arrange for her daughters to be forensically interviewed. They would take the investigation from this point.

The deputy received a call from the sergeant from the Special Victims Unit. The sergeant asked the deputy to fax a copy of his report to her. She said that detectives would handle the rest of the investigation.

The deputy called a case worker at the Child Protective Services and filed a report. He provided Anamarie with his police report number and the contact information for the Special Victims Unit sergeant. The deputy informed her that he notified Child Protective Services and they were aware of the situation.

The deputy completed his initial police report and turned it in to a supervisor. The case was then forwarded to the Maricopa County Sheriff's Office Special Victims Unit for further investigation.

Findings of the El Mirage Police Review

This case clearly warranted further investigation. Based on the statements of both girls the former live-in boyfriend could be charged with Indecent Exposure for the incident that occurred in the pool. The two girls needed to be forensically interviewed to determine whether their allegations were true. If the forensic examiner determined that the 12 year-old girl was telling the truth, the suspect should have been picked up and interviewed about touching her at night while she slept.

Even though the deputy's report indicates this case was sent to the Special Victims Unit, there is no documentation showing they did any follow up work on this crime. Apparently, it was never completed.

Live-in Boyfriends and Houseguests Who Molest Children

Many studies have been done which analyze incestual relationships between men and their "biological" children. These are often known as "intra-familial" relationships. That category also includes inappropriate relationships between children and other "blood relatives" (siblings, grandparents, etc.). Cases involving fathers who molest their "biological" children are covered in a different chapter of this book.

This chapter deals specifically with children who are sexually abused by men who are cohabitating in a "family" setting with the child's mother or family. These cases often involve the live-in boyfriend of the victim's mother or other family member.

Unfortunately, child molesting cases involving "live-in boyfriends" and other houseguests are not widely studied. They are one of the more common yet overlooked situations involving children who are molested in their own homes.

Even police departments don't track these offenders as a separate category. As a result, it is difficult to find many reliable statistics on this subject. Therefore, most of the information contained in this section is anecdotal and based on the experiences of victims, suspects, counselors and police officers. Although this subject may not be widely studied it is disturbingly frequent.

Not Truly Intra-Familial

The information included in this chapter deals with situations which may *seem* to be intra-familial but are not in the true meaning of the term. These situations occur within a "family unit" but the dynamics are very different.

These are not cases that involve child victims who are "blood" relatives of their offenders. These children are victims of circumstances that evolved through a relationship between their mother and the man she brought into their life. They are living under the same roof with a strange man which can create a multitude of problems – including inappropriate sexual conduct.

The information in this section is not meant to pass judgment or criticize women with children for cohabitating. Due to the high rate of divorce many couples are cohabitating for variety of reasons.

Relationships and family dynamics are a complex and diverse issue. Many factors may contribute to a single mom's decision to live with or marry a man. Love, loneliness, money, stability, companionship may all be factors she considers in her decision to cohabitate or marry.

Additionally, this information is not meant to infer that *all* live-in boyfriends molest their girlfriends' children. Clearly, some men are able to sustain a healthy and caring relationship with the children. Many are successful in developing a responsible "parent" role with the child and create a cohesive family environment.

But, experienced law enforcement officers know this is not always the case. There is clearly an ever-growing problem with children being molested by their mom's live-in boyfriend - especially young girls.

An El Mirage Police Report

CASE # 07-1050834
Child Molesting
Date: May 29, 2007
Victim: 3, 6, 8 and 9 year-old girls
Suspect: 35 year-old male

This case involves a woman and her four young daughters who were living with the woman's mother and new husband. Evidence suggested the girls were being molested by their new "step-grandfather." The police were called to investigate.

Here is the police report:

Facts of the Case:

On May 29, 2007 around 3:30 p.m. an El Mirage police officer was dispatched to a Family Health facility on Grand Avenue in El Mirage on a Child Molesting call.

When the officer arrived he contacted a nurse manager named "Phyllis." Phyllis told the officer there was a woman in the clinic by the name of "Margarita" who was there with her four daughters. Margarita was at the clinic because her daughters were complaining of pain in their vaginal areas and the mother suspected they were being molested.

The first child to be examined was 4 year-old "Generosa." When the little girl realized she was going to have her vaginal area checked she became very upset and started crying. The examining nurse had to nearly force the child's legs apart to conduct the examination. No trauma was observed in Generosa's genital area.

Phyllis told the officer that Margarita's 6 year-old daughter Selena disclosed to her that her step-grandfather "Reginato" puts his hand down her pants and touches her vaginal area. When Phyllis tried to obtain more information the child refused to talk anymore.

Margarita's other daughter, 9 year-old "Sonya" also disclosed to Phyllis that she had seen Reginato touch her 13 year-old aunt inappropriately. (Apparently, that incident occurred a few years earlier and was reported to the police. Reginato was subsequently arrested on a Child Molesting charge.)

Phyllis told the officer that Margarita and her daughters live with Margarita's mother "Christina" in a house on Ester Drive in El Mirage. Reginato is Christina's husband and he also lives in the house. Reginato is not a blood-relative to Margarita or any of her daughters.

The officer then contacted Margarita away from her children. She told the officer that for the past few months her daughters have been complaining of pain in their vaginal areas when she gives them baths. Margarita said she made sure the girls were kept clean in their private parts yet they continued to complain of pain and burning.

Margarita said that on May 28th her 6 year-old daughter Selena disclosed to her that Reginato had put his hand down her pants and put his finger in her vagina. At that point she was concerned about all of her daughters and decided to take them to the clinic to be examined.

Margarita told the officer that Reginato had a history of sexually abusing young girls. About three years ago he molested Margarita's 13 year-old sister in front of Margarita's daughter Sonya. He was arrested for that incident but was later released. Margarita said that Reginato even tried molesting her when she was younger. He also molested one of her mother's nieces.

Margarita provided the officer with a full description of Reginato including his birthday.

The officer called his supervisor to brief him about the situation. The sergeant responded to the officer's location to assist with the investigation. The supervisor contacted the sergeant from the Special Victims Unit and the case was assigned to a detective for follow up investigation.

The officer notified Child Protective Services and briefed them on the situation. He provided them with the address on Ester Drive where the child molesting allegedly occurred.

The on-scene police supervisor asked the attending physician at the health clinic to proceed with examining the other three girls. Following the examinations he told the officer that he found nothing significant in Selena's vaginal area. However, 8 year-old "Sophia's" genital area was red and had a light clear discharge; Sophia also complained of pain in that area. The doctor also reported that 9 year-old Sonya's genital area was unusually red and very swollen.

Marcella and her four daughters were transported to the Child Help facility in Phoenix for forensic exams. The Special Victims Unit detective met Marcella at the facility and took over the investigation.

The El Mirage officer completed his initial report and turned it in to his supervisor. The report was forwarded to the Special Victims Unit detective.

Findings of the El Mirage Police Review

This case was reviewed by the El Mirage Police Department in December 2007. The report did not include <u>any</u> information beyond the initial report by the El Mirage officer. There is no information that documents what if anything occurred at the Child Help facility or if the suspect was ever contacted, interviewed or arrested. There is no documentation that the investigation was ever completed by the Special Victims Unit.

The El Mirage police investigative staff contacted detectives, supervisors and command staff from the Maricopa County Sheriff's Office for clarification on whether the case had ever been completed. After weeks of repeated requests, the El Mirage investigators finally received a response from the sheriff's office saying they sent El Mirage their "entire report."

If that is the case, several unanswered questions remain. Where is the rest of the completed report? Were the four children forensically interviewed? Were the interviews documented? Was the suspect ever questioned about the allegations? Was that interview documented?

At this point those questions can only be answered by the Maricopa County Sheriff's Office.

How Does It Happen?

Clearly, most parents want their children to live in a stable, safe and secure home environment. Being a single parent often makes that seem difficult or impossible. For some single mothers one of the selling points to a live-in relationship might be the fact that her new partner can watch over her child while she is at work – child care.

Some child predators deliberately seek out and date women with the woman's children in mind. They will actually "target" women with young children with the sole purpose of molesting the children – especially young girls.

A woman with children should *always* give serious consideration to the "character" of a man before bringing him into their life. Obviously, this is easier said than done.

The age-old saying that *love is blind* still rings true today. But, it shouldn't dismiss a single mom's responsibility to provide a safe environment for her children. A woman in this situation should take reasonable steps to know the truth about a man's background. Is he a registered sex offender or have a history of child molesting or sex crimes? Has he been in jail or prison?

Some of the most dangerous situations are created by sexual predators who have access to their girlfriends' children. There are even reported cases of child molesters who use "marriage" to gain access to their wife's small children.

These child molesters not only exploit a child's sexuality but they also exploit the child's life situation as well. It is a cycle of behavior that is sometimes difficult for a child to escape.

As stated in other chapters, child molesters are very secretive. The same is true with live-in boyfriends or other houseguests who molest the children living in the home. They generally wait to be alone with the child - most often when the mother is at work.

They will use a variety of techniques to lure their victims. Because of the "family" dynamic of cohabitating with the mother and child, some live-in boyfriends will exploit their "adult authority" over the child, and use bribery, threats or even the false pretense of "sex education" to sexually abuse the child.

An abusive live-in boyfriend or houseguest may use a variety of techniques to avoid detection. They play on the child's sympathies or may even threaten the child into believing that the child and mother will be "homeless" without him. Some threaten to harm the child or mother if the child says anything.

Some of these situations begin when the child is very young. Others begin when the child starts to experience puberty.

At first many children may trust the boyfriend because their mother trusts him. This is only "natural" for the child because the mother allowed him to live in the same house with them. Children will generally trust their mother; therefore, if she says the man is trustworthy they will believe her.

In many cases the child's biological father is not around and the girl may be in need of male or "fatherly" companionship. All too often the live-in boyfriend not only will assume that role but will exploit the child's needs.

Like other child molesters, live-in boyfriends or other houseguests rarely use physical force against their victims.

They are more apt to use long term seduction techniques to gain the trust and confidence of the child before they begin touching them.

There are a variety of reasons why a child may be reluctant to disclose that their mother's boyfriend is abusing them. Some children are wiser than we give them credit for.

A young girl may have witnessed the breakup of her parents and have deep-felt sympathy for her mother. She may recognize that her mother has found "happiness" with the man she is with. The child may feel she will jeopardize her mother's happiness by disclosing what her live-in boyfriend is doing to her. She wants to see her mother happy so she remains silent.

The abuser may convince the child that it will be her fault if the offender gets in trouble for what he's doing. He may convince her that her mother and family will blame *her*. If the relationship ends between the mother and her boyfriend the child may feel guilty about creating a situation where the mom ends up alone.

There have even been reported cases where young girls believe they are "saving" their younger sister from being molested by their mom's live-in boyfriend. The offender convinces the girl that he will sexually abuse her younger sister instead of her if she resists him. The girl doesn't want that to happen to her little sister so she allows the molester to have his way.

One of the common strategies of many child molesters is to put fear into the minds of their victims. They often tell the child they will hurt them, their mother or their family. Sometimes they convince the child that a monster will get them if they tell anybody what he did to them. Others will tell the child what happened was the child's fault and they will get in trouble if anyone finds out.

An El Mirage Police Report

CASE # 07-1050828
Sexual Misconduct With a Minor
Date: February 1, 2007
Victim: 9 year-old female
Suspect: Adult male

This case involves a 9 year-old girl who disclosed to some schoolmates that she had been molested by her grandmother's live-in boyfriend. One of the schoolmates told a teacher and the police were called to investigate.

Here is the police report:

Facts of the Case:

On February 1, 2006 an El Mirage police officer was dispatched to a local elementary school in El Mirage on a report of a Sexual Misconduct with a Minor. When the officer arrived at the school he contacted the school counselor named "Jessie."

The counselor told the officer she was given an assignment by the school principal to follow up on an allegation made by one of their 5th grade girls and then take the appropriate action.

The 11 year-old girl named "Valencia" apparently told some of her schoolmates that she was sexually assaulted one time when she was 9 years old. The girl's friends reported what she said to a school tutor who in turn reported it to the school principal.

Jesse told the officer she called Valencia into her office to speak with her. She said the 5th grade girl told her that about two years ago she was asleep in her grandmother's living room. Valencia said she woke up and saw her grandmother's boyfriend "Paulo" standing over her wearing only his boxer shorts. She said Paulo then left the room.

Valencia told the counselor that Paulo returned a short while later. She said this time Paulo was completely naked and kneeled over her while she was lying on her back. The girl said that he tried to put his penis in her mouth but she wouldn't let him.

The counselor said the little girl told her she never told anyone about this until now. Apparently, Valencia was frightened and didn't know what to do so she just "kept it inside." The young girl told Jessie that Paulo is no longer together with her grandmother and she has not seen him in a long time.

The officer completed his report and notified his supervisor. The report indicates the case was assigned to the Special Victims Unit of the Maricopa County Sheriff's Office for follow up investigation on February 27, 2007.

Findings of the El Mirage Police Review

This case clearly warranted further follow up investigation by a detective. While the child may not have been in any immediate danger, she was still the victim of a child predator. The detectives should have arranged for a forensic interview of the young girl. If the forensic examiner determined her allegations were true the detectives could have tracked down and arrested the suspect.

However, there is no documentation in the report that shows the Special Victims Unit ever followed up on this case.

The Mother's Reaction

A woman who discovers her live-in boyfriend has molested her daughter may react in different ways. Some do the right thing – end the relationship and notify the authorities. Others disbelieve their own daughter and keep the relationship going. These women may be motivated by a variety of issues to have them react in that manner.

And sometimes a mother will even side with the man against her own children. Some do this for survival or money; others out of fear, denial or disbelief. This can cause inter-family relationship issues. It can divide families and make the child look bad for accusing the family's "provider."

Sometimes a mother will even lie to protect her live-in boyfriend. Others will force their own child to lie about what has happened to prevent jail or other consequences for the boyfriend.

When these extreme situations occur the "family dynamic" is completely shattered. The victimized child is often intimidated and made to feel responsible for the problems within the home. The child feels abandoned and overcome with fear, shame and despair.

Some mothers just simply ignore their daughter's accusations of sexual abuse. Others will subconsciously refuse to believe their boyfriend could be sexually involved with her own daughter - instead of her.

A mother's disbelief can be devastating to the child and cause the child to react in different ways. Some children will tell a trusting family member such as a grandparent. Most will simply live with the pain and fear. Others will run away from home. Others turn to drugs, alcohol and even suicide. Some will be emotionally traumatized for their entire life.

Relationships between a woman and a live-in boyfriend who molests her children rarely last. The true character of the boyfriend usually comes out and the woman eventually sees the light. By then a great deal of damage has usually occurred and the mother is left to deal with all of it.

Child abuse of girls by their mother's live-in boyfriend can extend for long periods of time if gone undetected. Some even extend into the victim's adulthood.

Prevention

Some facts are indisputable:

- A child is safest living in a home in which the biological parents are married.
- Situations of cohabitation increase the risk of child molesting.

Experts in child abuse prevention agree that parents can take steps to keep their children safe from sexual abuse and molesting. As mentioned in other chapters of this book, open and trusting communication is the best key to prevention and detection. Trusting conversations between parents and children will teach the children to be comfortable telling their parents most anything.

Parents should also teach their children about their body at a young age. The child should be told that no one is allowed to touch them on their private parts. Explain these things in terms the child can understand without scaring them.

Speak in age-appropriate terms when describing the child's body parts. Young children will feel more comfortable talking about them. Older children should be taught to speak about body parts in adult terms when appropriate. The key is for children of all ages to feel comfortable about talking about their body with their parents.

Parents should teach their children to respect themselves and demand respect from others. This will help a child to recognize if someone is treating them inappropriately. If something does happen the child will likely feel uncomfortable and react accordingly.

An El Mirage Police Report

CASE # 06-1050822
Child Molesting
Date: March 16, 2006
Victim: 13 year-old female
Suspect: 42 year-old male

This case involves a 13 year-old girl who disclosed to family members that her mother's new live-in boyfriend was molesting her at night while she sleeps in her bed. The police were called to investigate.

Here is the police report:

Facts of the Case:

On March 16, 2006 an El Mirage police officer was dispatched to a local elementary school in El Mirage in reference to a Child Molesting call. When the female officer arrived at the school she contacted a school counselor named "Jessie."

The counselor told the officer she received an e-mail that morning from the school principal asking her to contact one of their 8th grade students named "Yanina." The principal informed Jessie that Yanina's biological father "Geraldo" had come to the school and was very upset. Geraldo told the principal that he found out that his 13 year-old daughter was being molested by his ex-wife's new live-in boyfriend "Franco."

Geraldo said his daughter was visiting her grandmother over the weekend. Apparently, the young girl confided in her grandmother and aunt that her mother's boyfriend had been touching her inappropriately. Yanina's grandmother in turn notified Geraldo about it.

The principal wanted Jessie to talk to Yanina about the situation and then take the appropriate measures.

Jesse told the officer she called Yanina into her office to speak with her. Yanina was very uncomfortable at first but eventually told the counselor what was going on at home.

Yanina said that several weeks ago she was asleep in her bedroom at home. She was suddenly awakened and found her mother's boyfriend Franco rubbing her breasts and stomach area with his hands over her pajamas. Yanina said Franco then started rubbing her "front and back area." The girl asked Franco what he was doing and he told her he was looking for her mother's cell phone and then walked out of the room. Yanina said this happened around 2:00 a.m. when everyone was asleep.

Yanina told the school counselor that "other things" have also happened with Franco. The girl said that about a month ago she was sound asleep but then awakened to find Franco leaning over in the middle of the night. Yanina said this happens late at night all the time - at least twice a week. Each time she asks Franco what he is doing near her. And each time he tells her he is looking for her mother's cell phone and then leaves the room.

The girl said she tried to tell her mother what Franco was doing to her but her mother didn't believe her. Yanina said her mother told her it's her own fault if Franco was doing those things to her.

The counselor told the officer that when she asked Yanina more direct questions about what Franco was doing to her, the girl became withdrawn, displayed "uncomfortable *body language" and began picking on her fingernails. Jessie also said she was very concerned for Yanina's welfare because the girl told her she was afraid at home.*

Jessie said she notified Child Protective Services about what Yanina had disclosed to her and was told to notify the police.

The officer completed her report and notified her supervisor. The El Mirage officer faxed a copy of her report to the Special Victims Unit of the Maricopa County Sheriff's Office for follow up investigation.

Findings of the El Mirage Police Review

This was another case that should have been handled immediately by a detective. If the allegations were true, this young girl was living in a dangerous environment. Her mother didn't seem to believe her and the live-in boyfriend was still there. The victim expressed to the school counselor that she was afraid at home.

A Maricopa County Sheriff detective was faxed the report in March 2006. However, it appears that the detective did not complete the investigation and it was returned to El Mirage in 2007.

Warning Signs

Many times the warning signs are already there and a mother can usually sense when something is wrong. She may "know" or suspect something is not right between her boyfriend and her daughter. How he looks at the girl, what he says to her, how he touches her. Do they appear to be hiding "secrets?" Whether the mother ignores those signs or acts upon them will generally determine what happens to her child.

Conversely, a mother should never be fooled by the appearance of an otherwise "normal" looking relationship between her boyfriend and her daughter. It is not uncommon for a child to be molested in secrecy and then carry on normal, even recreational activities with her abuser. Some young girls who are molested at night are able to play games with the man during the day.

Some mothers don't know the signs or they overlook or misinterpret a child's cries for help. If your daughter tells you she doesn't want to be alone with a particular man there is probably a good reason and it should never be ignored. A child who displays unusual fear of a man even though they should be familiar with them (over time) is a clear sign that something is wrong.

Mothers with live-in boyfriends should never ignore these obvious warning signs. If your daughter tells you she feels "uncomfortable" around your boyfriend do not simply _dismiss_ the claim. Listen to what your daughter is saying and ask questions.

Parents are also warned against falling into the "Crying Wolf" denial mode. Just because the child lied or embellished a past allegation doesn't necessarily mean she is lying again. Gather all the facts before dismissing her allegation.

Another warning sign – especially with younger children is if they begin removing their clothes at night. This behavior should trigger a mother to ask more questions of the child.

A child who begins wetting the bed could be another warning sign. Other emotional issues could also cause this nighttime behavior but the possibility of molesting should never be overlooked.

As cruel as it sounds, some molesters will tell a child there is a "monster" hiding in her bedroom closet. They convince the child that the monster will only come out if they tell someone what he did to her. As a result, the child may have trouble sleeping and tell her mother that there is a "monster" hiding in her closet. Ask questions about who told her about the monster and why.

A child may also become "clingy" with her mother and at the same time avoid the boyfriend. This is another sign that something may not be right.

Parents should also be alerted to certain words and phrases used by children. Some of these phrases might be an indicator that something unusual is occurring.

Key phrases (or variations of phrases) to watch for:

- "He plays a game with me. . ."

- "My mother's boyfriend likes. . ."

- "I don't like to be alone with him. . ."

- "A monster's gonna get me. . ."

- "I'm afraid to go home. . ."

- "Sometimes he hurts me. . ."

Another clue might be if the child begins having unexpected problems in school including poor grades or behavioral notices. Newly developed behavioral issues around the home are also a telltale sign of abuse. Inappropriate outbursts of anger or a negative attitude might also be signs to watch for.

An obvious warning sign is complaints of soreness or irritation in a child's private areas. A more subtle sign would be if a young girl starts frequently changing her underwear because she feels "dirty" in her private area.

A noticeable decline in the girl's self-esteem is also a possible clue she is being molested. Emotional or personality changes such as a child belittling herself and openly questioning her self-worth are also causes for concern. In extreme cases a girl who is being molested might display behavioral changes such as hitting or injuring herself.

Another clue – especially with younger girls – is if they ask their mother or someone else to touch their private area. This is a "learned behavior" and a clear indication of possible molesting. In these cases the child should be questioned about why they want to be touched there.

Another cause for concern should be if a young girl suddenly has a new "nickname" for her private areas. The child should be questioned as to who told her that name.

An El Mirage Police Report

CASE # 06-1050816
Sexual Assault
December 29, 2006
Victim: 15-year old female
Suspect: 15-year old male

This case involves a 15 year-old girl who was forced into non-consensual sex in her home with a 15 year-old male houseguest. The police were called to investigate.

Here is the police report:

Facts of the Case:

On December 29, 2006 an El Mirage police officer responded to a park near 121st Avenue and Corrine Ave. The officer was dispatched there on a report of a Sexual Assault.

When the officer arrived he contacted two women identified as "Marian" and "Theresa." After some discussion with the women the officer was able to determine that Theresa's 15-year old daughter "Melissa" had been forced into non-consensual sex on multiple occasions by a 15-year old live-in houseguest named "Brad."

After getting the basic story from the girl's mother the officer and a sergeant from the Maricopa County Sheriff's Office interviewed Melissa about what happened to her.

Melissa told the officers that 15-year old Brad was a friend of the family and had been staying in their home for a few weeks but was no longer staying there. Melissa said on numerous occasions Brad tried to coax her into having sex with him but she repeatedly refused.

Melissa told the officers that Brad persisted for five straight days and she finally gave in and had sex with him a few weeks ago. She said she did not want to but he wouldn't leave her alone and she didn't know what else to do.

Melissa said that a few days later Brad told her he wanted to have sex again. But, this time she refused. Melissa said that Brad forced himself on her anyway and had sexual intercourse against her will.

The officers learned that Brad apparently told Melissa that he would do it to her "whenever he wanted to." Melissa was troubled by this and confided in a male friend "Bobby" telling him what Brad was doing to her - that he had "raped" her. After hearing this Bobby contacted Melissa's mother to let her know what happened. That's when she notified the police.

The El Mirage police officer completed his initial report on the incident. The on-scene Maricopa County Sheriff's sergeant notified the supervisor of the Special Victims Unit and informed her of the situation. The report was then forwarded to the Special Victims Unit for follow up investigation.

Findings of the El Mirage Police Review

This case should have been handled immediately by a detective. If the allegations were true, this 15 year-old girl had been sexually assaulted. The identity of the suspect was known and he should have been interviewed about the allegations.

The Maricopa County Sheriff's Special Victims Unit was notified of this incident in December 2006. However, there is no documentation in the report that shows the detectives ever completed this case and it was returned to El Mirage in October 2007.

Respond Appropriately

It is important to remember that children who have been molested or abused are often confused and emotionally torn. Some may feel they did something wrong or they are somehow to blame for what happened to them. They may be *unwilling* to talk about the situation unless they are *comfortable* talking with their parents.

The physical surroundings where a parent talks to their child is also very important. Mothers who suspect a problem should talk to their children in *private* and certainly not in the presence of her boyfriend.

If you feel your child is being molested or touched inappropriately, talk to them immediately. Take them to a location where no one else is around where they will feel safe talking openly with you. Give them a *genuine* reassurance that it's OK to tell you anything and they should have no fear of any reprisal.

It is important that the child understands that whatever they tell you is *not their fault*. Convince the child you will protect them if someone has told them they would be hurt for disclosing something. The child must believe they are safe in telling you *anything*.

The most important thing is that you react *appropriately* as a parent and handle the situation correctly. Most kids are resilient. If handled properly through love and understanding, or even counseling if needed, most children will recover from their ordeal with little or no long term effects.

****

Chapter 11

Fathers Who Molest Their Biological Children

Chapter 11 includes *five* police reports describing situations in which men sexually abused their own biological children. The victims in these cases were four young girls between the ages of 3 to 14 years, and a 14 year-old boy. These five reports are among the dozens of investigations mishandled by the Maricopa County Sheriff's Office.

This chapter also provides detailed information on the psychological trauma and other clinical issues a child can endure from being sexually abused by their own biological father. It also describes the devastation this crime can have on an entire family.

El Mirage Police Report

CASE # 07-1050832
Child Molesting
Date: March 30, 2007
Victim: 13 year-old female
Suspect: 37 year-old male

This case involves a 13 year-old girl who ran away from home late one night. She went to a park in a neighboring city but became frightened. The girl called her uncle who picked her up at the park. She disclosed to the uncle that her father had been sexually molesting her. The police were called to investigate.

Here is the police report:

Facts of the Case:

On March 30, 2007 around 10:00 p.m. an El Mirage police officer was dispatched to a home in the 13900 block of North "B" Street on a call of a Runaway Juvenile. When the officer arrived he contacted 37 year-old "Lucero" who wanted to report his 13 year-old daughter "Xenia" as a runaway.

Lucero said that he and his wife left for work at 4:30 p.m. and Xenia was in her room. When they got home from work around 9:30 p.m. Xenia was gone. Lucero told the officer he spoke with his neighbors to see if anyone had seen Xenia. One of the neighbors said she saw the girl in front of her house right after Lucero and his wife left for work.

Lucero told the officer he knew of no reason why Xenia would run away from home.

The officer then completed his police report of the Missing/Runaway Juvenile and called the information about Xenia into the national law enforcement database N.C.I.C.

Shortly after 11:00 p.m. the officer was again dispatched to Xenia's home. When he arrived Lucero told him that Xenia was brought home by her uncle Lugo and she was safe. The officer then asked to speak with Lugo to find out where he found Xenia.

Lugo told the officer that his niece called him and said she had run away from home. She told him she was at a park in nearby Youngtown, Arizona. Xenia said she was scared and asked her uncle Lugo if he would pick her up. Lugo informed the officer he picked up Xenia at the park and drove her home.

The officer then spoke to Xenia to explain the dangers of running away from home and to ask her why she ran away.

Xenia told the officer she was alone at the park and had not been drinking, smoking or doing any "criminal stuff." She then disclosed to the officer the reason she ran away from home was because her father has been sexually touching her and kissing her.

She said this had been going on for some time. Xenia told the officer that a few months ago she was in her room and her father came in. She said he began rubbing her breasts and taking off her clothes. She said she mentally "blocked out" what he did to her after that.

Xenia said that a few days ago she was at the car wash in El Mirage and her father made her kiss him with her tongue. She told the officer that she tried to tell her mother what was going on but said she didn't believe her. Xenia said she felt the only way out was to run away from home.

At that point the officer stopped the interview and notified a supervisor about the situation. The sergeant notified the sergeant from the Maricopa County Sheriff's Office Special Victims Unit about the incident.

The officer notified a case worker at Child Protective Services to arrange for placement of Xenia in a safe foster home. Due to the late hour of the night, the case worker asked if Xenia could temporarily stay with a family member. Her uncle Lugo agreed to take Xenia home with him.

The officer then cancelled the Missing/Runaway Juvenile report from N.C.I.C. and completed the initial report on the Child Molesting. He turned the report into his supervisor and it was forwarded to the Special Victims Unit. The sergeant told the officer that the Special Victims Unit would handle the investigation from this point on.

Findings of the El Mirage Police Review

This was a serious case that warranted timely follow up by the detectives. The girl said she ran away because she didn't feel safe in her own home. The detectives needed to arrange for a forensic interview of the victim. If the forensic examiner deemed the girl was telling the truth, the victim's father needed to be arrested and brought in for questioning.

The Special Victims Unit was notified about this case when it was initially reported to the police. The officer sent a copy of his report to the detectives. However, it appears that the sheriff's detectives never completed the investigation.

Fathers Who Molest Their Biological Children

One of the deepest and darkest secrets within a family deals with children who are molested by their *biological* fathers. In some cultures females are held in "low" regard and young girls are molested by their fathers at a much higher rate than in the United States. But, in our society it is strictly taboo – and illegal.

Blood relatives who molest a family member are among a classification of sex offenders sometimes referred to as "intra-familial" offenders. This group also includes grandfathers, uncles and cousins of their victims.

As in most other situations of child molesting the sexual misconduct between a biological father and his child are always done in secret. They are almost always done through the misuse of power or authority over the child.

Most cases involve young girls being molested; however, some fathers also molest their own biological sons. Some children are less than a year old when they are first victimized by their father. Half of all victims are under the age of 10 years.

Human Sexuality

Human sexuality is a very complex and diverse phenomenon. Morality and human ethics are among the many factors that contribute to the manner in which we control our sexual desires.

Most everyone suffers with sexual temptations in their life. We all experience normal hetero or homo sexual attractions to other human beings.

Age-appropriate sexual attraction is normally healthy and socially acceptable. A person's character, their conscience and social mores all play a role in avoiding inappropriate temptations.

A controlled drive for sexual activity is natural and normal. Most humans control their sexual responses within their brain. A healthy attitude towards sex will help a person avoid promiscuity and other irresponsible sexual behavior.

However, some men fail to control their sexuality and develop inappropriate and sometimes unlawful sexual habits. When these levels reach a certain point they begin to disregard the fact they may even be hurting others. They ignore their conscience and their "right from wrong" responses give way to their sexual urges.

They will minimize the harm they create to their victims and will justify their actions. These men put their sexual urges above all else.

In our society sexual attraction to young children by an adult is considered an unacceptable perversion. If the adult acts upon his desires it becomes a serious criminal offense.

Most adults have a normal, healthy understanding of their sexuality. It is difficult for most of us, therefore, to understand how a father could be sexually attracted to his own biological child. Sexually abusing one's own child is unthinkable.

Innocence Destroyed

Most young girls lack the emotional maturity to understand or effectively handle being a molesting victim by her father. For a young boy, being molested by his own father is a very disturbing and sensitive situation.

From a child's perspective adult family members are role models. They are the "providers" for the family. Most young children view their father as a man who brings a sense of safety and comfort to the child within the home. It becomes a source of tremendous confusion when the man who is supposed to protect them is actually abusing them.

The discovery of this type of sexual abuse by a father will have a profound impact on the entire family.

El Mirage Police Report

CASE # 06-1122105
Child Molesting
April 10, 2006
Victim: 14-year old male
Suspect: 33 year-old biological father

This case involves a 14 year-old boy whose mother was in the process of divorcing the boy's father. As part of the court proceedings the father was seeking "visitation" rights with the boy. The 14 year-old disclosed that his father had had been touching him inappropriately for over a year. The police were called to investigate.

Here is the police report:

Facts of the Case:

On April 10, 2006 an El Mirage officer was dispatched to investigate a Child Molesting. The woman who wanted to make the report was waiting in the lobby of the El Mirage Police Department.

The officer contacted 33 year-old "Catherine" who said she wanted to report that her 33 year-old husband "Charles" had been touching their 14 year-old son "Nathan" inappropriately.

Catherine told the officer that approximately a year ago Nathan disclosed to her that his father was touching him inappropriately and it made him uncomfortable. Nathan told his mother that his father came in his bedroom recently and he was drunk. The boy said his father told him he "wanted to play." Catherine said that Nathan was uncomfortable in describing to her the details of what happened that night.

She told the officer that on more than one occasion she has walked in on her husband while he was "playing" with Nathan. She said Charles would pull the boy's pants down exposing his penis. Catherine said each time she yelled at her husband to stop doing that. Her husband would tell her it was OK they were just "wrestling."

Catherine said she had hoped the activity would stop but it never did. She said she recently told her husband he had to move out of the house and she was filing for divorce. During the proceedings she was told that Charles would have visitation rights and Nathan would have to spend some weekends with his father.

Nathan told his mother that he did not want to be alone with his father, but she told him a judge could order the visitation. Nathan said he would tell the judge that his father had been touching him inappropriately in the hopes to prevent visitation.

Catherine told the officer she believed her husband Charles had once been sexually assaulted or molested as a child which could be a reason for his deviant behavior. She also told the officer that Charles had been arrested six months earlier in Surprise, Arizona after he was "caught with a 15 year-old girl in the desert."

The officer did not interview Nathan. He knew the proper protocol was to have detectives schedule a forensic interview of the victim.

The officer notified Child Protective Services and briefed them on the situation. He completed his report and notified his supervisor. The officer told Catherine the case would be turned over to detectives and they would contact her.

The police report indicates the case was sent to the Special Victims Unit of the Maricopa County Sheriff's Office on May 3, 2006.

Findings of the El Mirage Police Review

This case showed cause for concern and required further investigation by detectives. The suspect in this case is the boy's biological father. According to his wife and police records he had a previous arrest for taking a 15 year-old girl into the desert.

The young victim was obviously traumatized over this situation and feared having to spend time alone with his father. A forensic interview of the victim should have been arranged to learn more specific details about the allegations he was making. If the examiner believed the allegations were true, the detectives should have picked up the suspect for questioning.

However, based on the information in the police report it appears that nothing more was ever done on this case by the Special Victims Unit detectives. The report does not include any explanation as to why the investigation was not completed.

Effects on the Family

When young boys or girls are molested by their biological father it often causes great emotional confusion for the child. They can easily become perplexed by the "strange" affection they are receiving from their father. The confusion will become even more profound as they get older and begin to understand the concepts of sex.

A child suffers tremendously from sexual abuse by their father. Not only from the psychological and physical trauma, but a young child can also be damaged by the emotional trauma of being sexually abused at a young age. But, there is also a stigma attached to the abuse - not just from the child's immediate family but also with their extended family.

The effects of child molesting by a biological father can unravel an entire family. When these immoral acts are disclosed, the victim's family may react with disbelief, shame and hurt. Not only is the relationship between the child and father destroyed, but it often destroys the relationship between the child's parents.

An incestual relation between a father and daughter can also drive a wedge between the child and her mother. Even the relationship between the child and her siblings can be affected.

A Father Forever

The effects of intra-familial sexual abuse for a victim are similar to those of other child molesting victims. They can suffer the same psychological and emotional issues.

But, the impact of a boy or girl being molested by their *own father* is usually more severe and recovery may last the child's entire life. The child may feel the effects long into adulthood. And, the ability to sustain a normal, healthy relationship may be forever effected by the image of their father molesting them.

In some respects sexual abuse committed by a stranger might be easier for a child to forget. The offender is generally removed from the child's life forever and time helps erase that bad memory.

But, when the offender is the child's own father, the burden on the victim is often inescapable. Some child victims become completely estranged from their fathers and go the rest of their life without contact with him.

In most cases, the child can never erase the fact that he will *always* be their father. He will always be present in their life either physically or through family history or discussions. This inescapable fact may prolong the healing process indefinitely.

When a child has been molested by their father, the untenable emotions are always present. This type of abuse causes a much deeper emotional trauma. Forgiveness becomes a delicate subject in the realm of emotional healing.

As in the case of other authority figures, a child is often confused by the actions of their father. They may feel self-blame, fear or shame as to what is happening to them. The child may feel compelled to keep the molesting a secret in order to maintain family unity. A molesting victim may also fear that they will not be believed because the appearance of the father's strong character.

\---

El Mirage Police Report

CASE # 07-1050829
Child Molesting
Date: March 25, 2007
Victim: 3 year-old female
Suspect: 24 year-old male

This case involves a 3 year-old girl whose mother noticed that the child's genital area was red and irritated and the child was complaining of pain. The little girl disclosed that her father had touched her inappropriately. A social worker found out about the sexual abuse and notified a Maricopa County Sheriff's deputy who started an investigation.

Here is the police report:

Facts of the Case:

On March 25, 2007 a Maricopa County Sheriff's deputy took a telephonic report in reference to a sexual abuse case that occurred in El Mirage, Arizona.

The deputy contacted a case worker from the Arizona Child Protective Services named "Alice." She told the deputy that in December of 2006 three-year-old "Pastora" told her mother "Marcella" that her father "Jorge" touched her and kissed her in her private areas. Marcella immediately confronted her husband about what the child had disclosed.

Marcella said Jorge broke down and started crying. He admitted to abusing their daughter but said he would never do it again.

A few days later 3 year-old Pastora was complaining of pain. Marcella looked at her daughter's private area and noticed it was red and irritated. Marcella was afraid to take Pastora to the hospital because she thought that Child Protective Services would take her daughter away.

Marcella said she leaves her daughter with Jorge every day between 2-10 p.m. when she is at work. Jorge is apparently in the United States illegally. According to Alice the entire family speaks only Spanish.

Alice told the deputy she went to the home on March 24th to check welfare on Pastora. She said that both Jorge and Marcella were at the house when she got there. Alice said she told Marcella that Jorge could no longer stay at the house alone with Marcella because of an allegation of abuse. Marcella then told Jorge to leave.

Alice told the detective she would need assistance in arranging for a forensic interview of the child.

The deputy completed his report and notified the supervisor of the Maricopa County Sheriff's Office Special Victims Unit. He also faxed a copy of his report to the sergeant.

Findings of the El Mirage Police Review

The facts of this case are very disturbing. A 3 year-old girl had physical evidence she had been sexually molested. The girl's father admitted he had molested the child. This case should have been handled immediately by a detective to ensure the child was not in danger.

The detective should have arranged for a forensic interview of the child. If the forensic examiner determined her allegations were true the detective could have tracked down and arrested the girl's father.

The report indicates the Special Victims Unit was notified about the incident and was sent a copy of the report. However, it appears that they never completed this case and it was returned to El Mirage in 2007.

Failure to Disclose

As described in other chapters some sexually abused children will not disclose their experience out of *fear*.

Their fear may be based on actual threats made by their offender, fear of reprisals from their family or fear they won't be believed.

Some children withhold information because they feel a need to *protect* their mother or the family structure.

Still others will not disclose they have been molested due to "dissociation." This generally means that the victim's normal cognitive thinking has been altered or disrupted. The child represses the abuse they have suffered from their conscious awareness. In layman's terms, they simply push the abuse right out of their mind. Some will remain silent for many years.

In some cases, a child may not disclose they are being molested because they feel disenfranchised from their family. They simply feel alone and have no one to talk to about it. This is typically the case when a young girl has been labeled as a "problem child" or is estranged from her mother or family.

The Mother's Denial

When a mother discovers that her child has been molested by her husband, it is important that she immediately does the right thing - protect the child and notify the authorities.

But this is not always the case. For variety of reasons some families decide to handle the situation "within" the family and keep it a secret. Reasons might include the father's immigrations status; protecting the family's "image" in the community; and, even shame or fear.

Some women may see signs and "suspect" something is amiss yet turn a blind eye to the evidence. Even after disclosure by their daughter, a woman may *still* refuse to believe her husband has sexually abused their child.

In some cases, a mother's "denial" may be based upon fear of violence or other extreme reaction from her husband. It is not uncommon for some mothers to feel a deep-rooted anxiety over being left alone if the husband is forced to leave. As a result, they place the needs of the victimized child behind their personal needs and fail to handle the situation properly.

Some mothers even blame their daughter for "family issues" that result in her husband sexually molesting the girl. This is typically the case when the relationship between the mother and daughter has been strained, or when marital or intimacy issues exist between the husband and wife.

Denial by the victim's mother may take another form. She may try to convince herself that her husband will stop molesting their child. But, that is rarely the case - the fathers most always reoffend.

If the mother doesn't handle the situation properly it shifts the burden back onto the child victim. This only compounds the emotional damage to the victim.

El Mirage Police Report

CASE # 06-1050813
Child Molesting
December 7, 2006
Victim**:** 8-year old female
Suspect: Victim's biological father

This case involves an 8 year-old girl who was visiting her grandmother in California and disclosed that her father had sexually molested her when she was staying with him in El Mirage, Arizona. The grandmother notified the authorities and an El Mirage police officer began an investigation.

Here is the police report:

Facts of the Case:

On December 7, 2006 the victim's grandmother "Lacy" called the El Mirage Police Station from her home in Long Beach, California. She spoke to a female officer and reported that her two granddaughters ("Brianna" age 8, and "Tammy" age 6) had come to live with her a couple months earlier in October 2006. Lacy informed the officer she has temporary legal guardianship of both girls.

The grandmother said that a few weeks earlier 8-year old Brianna told her that her father "James" had done "something bad" to her. The little girl was afraid to say because her father told her he would "have to go to jail" if she told anybody what he did. When Lacy insisted that Brianna tell her exactly what her father had done the little girl said, "He touched me." Lacy told the officer that she asked Brianna where her father had touched her and her granddaughter pointed to her vagina. The alleged molesting took place when Brianna was still living with her father in El Mirage, Arizona.

Lacy said she called the Child Protective Services in California and spoke with a case agent named "Tang." The grandmother gave the El Mirage officer the full name and contact information for the case worker in California.

The grandmother told the officer that the case agent had started an investigation in California. Apparently, a forensic interview and examination had already been scheduled by Child Protective Services agent. However, Agent Tang told Lacy that before she could proceed with the interview and examination she needed to make a police report.

So, Lacy said she went to the Long Beach Police Department. After hearing what had happened, the Long Beach police officer told Lacy that because her granddaughter had been molested in El Mirage, Arizona, the Long Beach police did not have jurisdiction. The officer told Lacy to call the El Mirage Police Department and file a police report with them.

Lacy told the El Mirage officer that Agent Tang had already contacted Arizona Child Protective Services about the case. She also told the officer that Agent Tang told her he had interviewed both girls and said she didn't believe Brianna's little sister had been molested.

After receiving the report from the victim's grandmother, the El Mirage officer tracked down the little girl's mother "Linda" in Arizona. Linda said she was recently divorced from the victim's father (James) and there is a restraining order in place. She said she and James actually have three daughters – Brianna, Tammy and 2 year-old "Missy." Linda told the officer she was being evicted from her residence and sent her two older daughters Brianna and Tammy to live with her mother Lacy in Long Beach in early October 2006.

According to Linda, her ex-husband still had visitation rights with their 2 year-old daughter Missy until a few weeks earlier when Brianna reported the molesting to her grandmother. Linda told the officer that an Arizona Child Protective Services case worker was now involved and James was no longer allowed to visit his daughter Missy. Linda provided the officer with the Arizona case worker's name and phone number.

After talking with the victim's mother, the El Mirage officer ran a "Premise History" check on the address in El Mirage where the molesting occurred. The officer found an extensive criminal history check on the girl's father. On December 8, 2006 the officer finalized her initial report of this Child Molesting and forwarded it to the Maricopa County Sheriff's Office Special Victims Unit.

On December 15, 2006 an El Mirage police sergeant received a phone call from California Child Protective Services (actually called California Department of Children & Family Services) Case Agent Tang inquiring about the status of this case. Agent Tang said she had interviewed the victim and had some useful information for the investigating detective.

The sergeant explained to Tang that the case had been forwarded to the Special Victims Unit at the sheriff's office and they would be handling the case. The sergeant gave the case agent the contact information for the Special Victims Unit.

The El Mirage sergeant documented this contact with Agent Tang in a supplemental police report.

Findings of the El Mirage Police Review

A review of the facts of this case indicates the victim's grandmother reported this felony crime of Child Molesting to the El Mirage Police Department on December 7, 2006. The case was ultimately assigned to a Maricopa County Sheriff's Office detective who conducted only a minimal amount of follow up investigation.

The 8-year old victim had been interviewed by a forensic interviewer at the Child Help facility in Phoenix some six months later on May 19, 2007. The interview was audio and video recorded and a tape of the interview was reportedly impounded as evidence in the Maricopa County Sheriff's Office evidence facility. Based on the police report provided by the sheriff's office it appears that nothing more was ever done on this case.

The tape-recorded interview revealed that the 8-year old girl had been molested by her natural father over a two-year period of time.

In early 2008 an El Mirage investigator re-opened the case and determined that the suspect was still serving time in the Arizona State Prison for an unrelated conviction for Armed Robbery. Although his whereabouts were known to the Maricopa County Sheriff's Office investigators at the time, it appears that the suspect in this case was never interviewed about molesting his daughter.

Based on the information in the police report this was clearly a prosecutable case and warranted further follow up by detectives. The Maricopa County Sheriff's Office report does not include any explanation as to why the case was not worked or worked timely to be submitted for prosecution.

Theories

There are as many theories about fathers who molest their biological children as there are studies about the subject. From those who study this issue, not many conclusions are drawn between men who *do* or *don't* molest their own children. Many of the same characteristics exist between both groups of men. However, those who sexually abuse their sons and daughters are clearly different when it comes to their moral character.

Some theorists conclude that it is a consequence of a society that gives a father "power" over his family.

Unquestionably, responsible parents need to extend some power or authority over their children. Teaching children and fairly disciplining them is part of the parent's role to create and maintain a strong family unity. "Parental power" is also necessary for the parents to instill strong character and integrity in their children.

But, abusing that power to sexually molest their own child is reprehensible. The father not only betrays the trust of his child but he takes advantage of the child's innocence and dependence upon him as an authority figure and role model.

The roles become confusing for a young girl being molested by her father. The man she has always looked up to and felt secure around is now violating her. Does she tell someone or continue to suffer the abuse? This internal conflict within the child may seem overwhelming.

A few far-reaching studies actually *remove* or *minimize* the primary blame from the offending father.

They suggest that a father will sexually turn to his daughter when his wife is no longer willing, able or interested in engaging in sex with him. Rather than turn his sexual needs outside the home he will turn to his own daughter. This theory attempts to place some of the "blame" for his sexual deviancy on his wife.

A similar theory actually blames the *child* for the father's sexual abuse. These theorists claim the child was cute or attractive and became "seductive" with age. As a result, the father's "innocent" signs of physical affection simply evolve into sexual contact. In essence, this theory blames the child for her father's abuse.

But, most theories conclude that fathers who sexually abuse their biological children are *child molesters*. They display many of the same traits as all molesters. Investigators often uncover a secret history of sexual perversion and pornography in the father's past.

Regardless of which theory makes the most sense, the bottom line is molesting your biological child is perverse and deviant. Fathers who sexually abuse their own children are *child molesters* – plain and simple.

It is very difficult for most of us to comprehend the depravity of a father sexually molesting his own child. Theorists can conjure up explanations for the causes but it does not excuse the fact the father's actions are sexually perverse and criminal.

Thankfully, the criminal justice system does not acknowledge any specific "theory of blame" in dealing with child molesters. The law doesn't differentiate between a blood relative, an acquaintance or a complete stranger. They are all treated equally as sex offenders.

A Child's Reaction

Child molesting victims react in a variety of different ways. A child molested by a priest might react different than a child molested by the soccer coach. A child victimized by a baby sitter might respond differently than a child molested by their father. Many factors contribute to the manner in which the child will react.

Many young victims have difficulty disclosing they have been molested or sexually abused. Some remain silent out of shame or fear.

Some girls are even reluctant to expose their abuser because of their *love* for him. This is sometimes the case when a young girl is molested by her biological father. These young victims become emotionally torn between disclosing their pain and protecting their offender.

A molested child may be more reluctant to disclose she has been molested by a *non-family* member than she would if the offender was a close family member. She may feel more fearful or apprehensive of the stranger.

Children who have been victimized from a very early age may not even recognize their situation is abnormal or wrong until they are much older. By that time their feelings and emotions may be paralyzed with confusion.

The abusive father may demand unconditional obedience from his daughter which can extend well beyond childhood and into later life. Young female victims often comply with their father due to fear and parental "respect." Some young girls may even feel loyalty to their abusive father as well as a sense of dependency for his protection.

Some long-time victims even believe that revealing their father's abuse would constitute an act of "betrayal" of the most significant person in their life. The father typically still exerts some control over the child in cases of long term sexual abuse. The child may become psychologically or emotionally dependent upon her abuser – particularly when it is her father.

Similar to cases of sexual abuse of children by live-in boyfriends, a biological father may exploit his daughter by trying to disguise his actions as "sex education."

In extreme cases of sexual abuse, a biological father may isolate the child from the rest of her family and friends by restricting her from activities beyond his control. The sexually abusive father may excessively punish the child for even minor infractions. These children live in constant fear of reprisal from their father and often live a life of limited interaction with outsiders. As a result they often become social outcasts or socially awkward among their own age group.

El Mirage Police Report

Case # 06-1050808
Child Molesting
May 15, 2006
Victim: 3-year old female
Suspect: Victim's biological father

This case involves a 3 year-old girl whose parents were divorced. When the child returned home following a visit with her father she disclosed that her father had been sexually molesting her. The police were called to investigate.

Here is the police report:

Facts of the Case:

On May 19, 2006 a uniformed El Mirage Police patrol officer was dispatched to a home on west Northview Drive in the neighboring city of Surprise, Arizona. The call was in reference to a possible Child Molesting of a 3 year-old girl.

When the El Mirage officer arrived at the residence he was contacted by a Surprise Police officer. The officer told him that the victim's mother "Lolita" spoke only Spanish. Lolita was reporting that her 3 year-old daughter "Yolanda" disclosed to her that she was touched inappropriately by her father. While questioning the mother further the Surprise officer determined that the offense had actually occurred at the home of the victim's father in El Mirage. At that point the El Mirage officer took over the investigation.

The El Mirage officer, who is a fluent Spanish-speaker, interviewed Lolita in more detail. The mother said that Yolanda was picked up by her biological father "Manfredo" on May 15, 2006 around 9:00 a.m. Manfredo had picked up his daughter as part of his parental visitation rights. According to Lolita he brought Yolanda home the next morning close to 9:00 a.m.

Lolita told the officer that around noon on May 19, 2006 she and her daughter were laying in Lolita's bed watching television. At one point, Yolanda took hold of her mother's hand and tried to guide it toward Yolanda's vaginal area. Lolita said she asked her daughter why she was doing that. At first the 3-year old was hesitant to answer her mother but finally Yolanda told her, "My daddy always does this to me." The mother said her daughter repeatedly tried to guide Lolita's hand towards Yolanda's vagina saying, "Do this to me." At that point Lolita said she called the police.

Lolita told the officer that this type of behavior had never occurred before and that she was very concerned about her daughter. She provided the officer with her ex-husband's information including his date of birth, physical description, home address in El Mirage, cell phone number and place of employment. Lolita told the officer that Manfredo lives with his current wife along with three children – all young girls.

The officer asked Lolita if she had already confronted Manfredo about Yolanda's disclosure that he molested her. She told the officer she had not said anything to him about it. The officer advised her not to discuss the investigation with Manfredo until further notice.

An El Mirage Police sergeant arrived on the scene and the officer explained the situation to the supervisor. The officer informed Lolita that she would be contacted by a Maricopa County Sheriff's detective for follow up on the case.

The El Mirage officer completed his initial police report and turned it in. The report was reviewed by an El Mirage supervisor and then forwarded to the Special Victims Unit for further investigation.

Findings of the El Mirage Police Review

This was a very serious allegation given the age of the victim and the alleged suspect being her biological father. There were three other young girls living in her father's current home that added to the urgency to resolve this case quickly and accurately.

In November 2007 an investigator from the "new" El Mirage Police Department examined this case. The facts in this case clearly show that immediate follow up by detectives was needed. However, based on the content of the police report it appears the Special Victims Unit never completed the case.

These types of allegations by small children against a parent are extremely difficult to prove or disprove and investigating them in a strategic and timely manner is critical.

If the allegation was true then the victim's biological father is likely a child predator of the worst kind. If the allegation by the child was false then law enforcement had an obligation to help clear the father's name.

One of the first steps should have been a "forensic interview" of the 3-year old girl. The forensic examiner could have rendered an opinion as to whether the little girl was telling the truth.

Another immediate step in the investigation should have been a "confrontation call" with the victim's father. Due to the fact that he was unaware that his daughter had disclosed the allegation, a "confrontation call" may have had a good chance of success.

This apparently incomplete investigation leaves many disturbing questions unanswered. The police report does not include any explanation as to why the case was not completed by the Special Victims Unit.

The Impact on the Victim

Some child victims develop a series of emotional coping mechanisms to deal with their situation. One of the more common techniques is to simply *ignore* the reality of her abuse – to deny its existence. By refusing to consciously acknowledge she is being violated a child can better cope with her pain, humiliation and fear.

In some cases the denial is so pronounced that the child cannot even admit her abuse when the offender has been caught in the act or is otherwise exposed. Some abusers will even shame their victims into believing they are to blame.

Some theories conclude that abusive tendencies are acquired through personal experiences – that abused children tend to grow up to be abusers themselves. This is based on the premise that children grow up and subconsciously seek to emulate their own childhood relationships and surroundings. This may explain why some girls who were abused as a child tend to gravitate towards abusive men as adults.

Issues with intimacy as they get older are one of the most common problems associated with child abuse victims. Their difficulty or inability to trust becomes a substantial hindrance in sustaining a lasting relationship.

Research shows that a surprising number of fathers who molest their biological children are staunchly conservative and traditionalists. Some profess to be devoutly religious and highly moralistic. Quite often they struggle with normal social relationships.

Many cases of sexual abuse by a biological father are found in problem marriages. The husband often has a very domineering personality. He may be abusive to his wife as well as sexually abusive towards his daughter.

Psychological Effects

Some statistics indicate that child victims of sexual abuse are less likely to marry or remain married. Sexually abused children may have difficulty understanding and managing their own sexuality as an adult. The extent, duration and severity of the abuse will have a direct impact on the child's ability to successfully recover from their ordeal.

Some psychologists believe that women who have been sexually assaulted as an *adult* have a better chance of successfully recovering from their ordeal than a child victim. Adults have a better understanding of the healing process and higher capacity to expunge traumatic experiences from their psyche. A sexually abused child cannot easily regain a sense of trust in humanity and may find difficult in sustaining meaningful relationships as an adult.

A Child's Recovery

Every victim of sexual abuse responds differently to treatment and counseling. A child who has been sexually abused by a biological parent needs professional help as soon as possible. The sooner a child receives proper treatment the sooner the physical and emotional healing will begin.

But there is more than just the emotional healing that must occur. There is also a relationship adjustment between all members of the family that will follow this situation. The reaction by members of the child's inner family has a lot to do with the healing process and how well the child copes with the situation.

Time also has a hand in the healing process. When the abuse is terminated at an early age, the victim has a better chance of total recovery. The extent of the emotional trauma endured by the victim will have a direct impact on her ability to successfully recover and live a normal life.

But, many victims of child molesting grow up to live mostly normal lives. Once they've overcome the stigma and other intra-familial issues related to the situation they generally cope with their past and move into productive adulthood.

****

Chapter 12
Sexual Assault

Chapter 12 includes *six* Sexual Assault police reports that were among those mishandled by the Maricopa County Sheriff's Office. The victims of these crimes were all girls between the ages of 12 and 17 years. Each of them was sexually assaulted by a stranger or an acquaintance.

Also included is statistical information about the crime of Sexual Assault. The chapter also describes how sexual assaults are investigated and prosecuted in court. Suggestions to avoid becoming a victim of sexual assault, the treatment and recovery for victims and recent legislation to assist sex-crime victims are also included.

El Mirage Police Report

CASE # 07-1050838
Sexual Assault
Date: June 25, 2007
Victim: 14 year-old female
Suspect: 16 year-old male

This case involves a 14 year-old girl who was at a house visiting some friends. She left to walk home and was accompanied by a 16 year-old male acquaintance from the neighborhood. On the way home the male sexually assaulted the girl in a nearby field. A Maricopa County Sheriff's deputy was called to investigate.

Here is the police report:

Facts of the Case:

On June 25, 2007 around 10:00 p.m. a Maricopa County Sheriff's deputy responded to a home in the 12700 block of W. Port au Prince Avenue in El Mirage on a report of a forcible Sexual Assault on a minor. The Maricopa County Sheriff's Office was under contract to provide police service to El Mirage so a sheriff's deputy was summoned to handle the call.

When the deputy arrived he contacted the 14 year-old victim's mother "Latoya." Latoya told the deputy that her daughter "Hope" came home that evening and told her she "needed to tell me something." Hope told her mother that she had been assaulted and "raped" by a 14-16 year-old acquaintance she knew only as "Aldo." Hope first met Aldo when she moved to El Mirage in April 2007.

Latoya told the deputy that she didn't have any more specific information about the attack but she did want Aldo prosecuted for assaulting her daughter.

The deputy asked Hope if she could point out the exact location where she was attacked. She then accompanied the deputy in his patrol car to show him where Aldo assaulted her.

The deputy then collected the clothing Hope had been wearing when she was attacked. The clothing would be impounded it as evidence and for forensic examination. He also notified his supervisor of the situation. According to the report the sergeant notified the Maricopa County Sheriff's Office Special Victims Unit.

Latoya then drove her daughter to a Phoenix-area hospital for an examination. The deputy sheriff completed a written police report on his contact with the victim and his mother.

That evening an El Mirage police officer contacted Hope at the hospital and obtained more specific information about the attack. Hope told the officer that she had been visiting a friend named "Josh" who lived a few blocks from her home. She said Aldo and a couple other acquaintances were also there. Hope told the officer that she decided to walk home around 7:00 p.m. and Aldo accompanied her.

Hope said that as they were walking home Aldo suddenly tackled her to the ground in the street. She said she "broke away" and started to run from Aldo. Hope said she ran to a dirt lot behind an abandoned mobile home and tried to hide. Aldo caught up to her and put her in a "head lock."

She said that Aldo threw her to the ground again and this time tried to pull her pants down. Hope said she tried to fight him off but he was too strong and she couldn't do it. Hope said she tried to scream for help but Aldo put his hand over her mouth and told her to "be quiet." Hope said that Aldo pulled her pants down and forcibly put his penis inside of her.

Hope said she knows that Aldo lives in her residential complex but she doesn't know exactly where. She said that Aldo and Josh are friends and Josh probably knows where Aldo lives.

The officer told Hope and her mother that Hope would need to take forensic medical exam at a specialized facility for victims of sexual assault. Latoya drove her daughter to the facility and the officer met them there. When they arrived a Maricopa County Sheriff's detective was there and the officer briefed him on what had occurred.

The officer then left the facility and completed his initial report on the incident. His report and that of the deputy sheriff who originally responded to the call were forwarded to the Special Victims Unit.

Findings of the El Mirage Police Review

This was a very serious case of a 14 year-old girl who had been sexually assaulted in her own neighborhood. Based on the young girl's allegation she was assaulted and forcibly raped. The identity of the suspect and his whereabouts were known. According to the report, a detective responded to the hospital to take over the investigation.

However, according to the police report the investigation was never completed. In early 2008, an El Mirage detective contacted a sheriff's sergeant about this case. The detective was told the case had been "closed" by the Special Victims Unit. There was no documentation that the sheriff's detectives had done anything further with this investigation. The report only indicated they had "Exceptionally Cleared" the case and closed it.

Sexual Assault

The term *sexual assault* has different connotations. Sexual assault includes those acts in which a person is made to engage in sexual acts through the use of physical force, threats, fear or coercion. By and large, nearly all sexual assaults are committed by men.

Most people think of sexual assault in the traditional form of *forcible rape*. But, sexual assault also includes other *non-consensual* sexual acts such as intercourse, sodomy, oral sex and others. Sexual assault also includes situations where the victim has been drugged or otherwise incapacitated and *unknowingly* engages in sexual acts.

Any form of sexual assault can be devastating to the victim. It is the ultimate personal violation for a human to be forced to engage in sexual acts against their will and *without their consent*.

The criminal codes in most states have replaced the term *Rape* with *Sexual Assault*. The term encompasses a broader spectrum of sexual offenses for purposes of prosecution.

Sexual Assault Offenders

People who commit sexual assault come from many different walks of life and different ages. Many have good jobs, are outstanding students and even active in their church.

There is an old saying that opportunity does not make a rapist. Most people will not commit a sexual assault simply due to circumstances. The decision to sexually assault another person comes from a much deeper cause. Most men control their sexual desires and express them through healthy and lawful outlets.

Sex offenders have difficulty controlling their urges and tend to be sexually impulsive. They rarely consider the consequences of their actions or the pain they are inflicting upon their victims.

Sexual assault is a widely studied crime and many theories exist as to why men commit sexual assault. Most studies conclude that sexual assault is a "learned behavior" and that many sex offenders had been victimized at some time in their lives.

Many have been hardened by their experience and are unable to relate to the feelings and emotions of their victims. A psychological barrier precludes them from understanding or appreciating that they are causing the *same* type of pain they once endured from a sex offender.

Sexual assault is not always committed simply for sexual gratification. It isn't always associated with passion or desire.

It is sometimes committed by men out of a subconscious need to dominate their victim. Others do it to abuse or humiliate the victim due to some pent up aggression or other dysfunctional issue.

Some theories conclude that the violent acts of sex offenders are a reaction to deep feelings of personal inferiority. They use violence and sexual attacks to express power and domination over their victims. This is often the case of sexual assaults by strangers, and particularly in the case of "serial" rapists who stalk a community.

Another theory draws the opposite conclusion. Some men with an overinflated sense of self-worth are sex abusers. They often feel superior to their victim.

This type of sex offender usually believes his victim holds far less "human value" than himself. He feels he can act out his sexual aggression on the victim without consequence. These offenders are often spousal abusers, bosses and others in leadership roles.

El Mirage Police Report

CASE # 07-1122106
Sexual Assault
June 11, 2007
Victim: 13-year old female
Suspect: Unknown adult male

This case involves a 13 year-old mildly retarded girl who was home alone when a stranger knocked at the door. He told the girl his car had broken down and needed to use her phone. Once inside the home the stranger sexually assaulted the young girl. A Maricopa County Sheriff's deputy was called to investigate.

Here is the police report:

Facts of the Case:

On June 11, 2007 around 11:00 a.m. a deputy from the Maricopa County Sheriff's Office responded to a call of a Sexual Assault at a residence in the 12700 block of West Port au Prince Avenue in El Mirage. The Maricopa County Sheriff's Office was under contract to provide police service to El Mirage so a sheriff's deputy was summoned to do the investigation.

When the deputy arrived he contacted the victim's mother "Leslie" who told him that her 13 year-old daughter "Darlene" had disclosed to her she had been sexually assaulted in their home sometime in the last 30 days. Leslie told the officer that Darlene is mildly retarded and being treated by a therapist at a local mental health facility.

Darlene told her that an unknown White man in his 30's with "scraggly hair" came to the front door of their residence and told her his car had broken down. The stranger asked if he could use the phone and bathroom. Darlene thought it would be OK and allowed the man into their home.

Once the man was in the residence, Darlene walked in her bedroom while he used the bathroom. When she came back into the living room a few minutes later the man hit her on the back of her head knocking her unconscious.

Darlene told her mother when she woke up the man was gone. She was lying on her bed with her panties pulled down to her ankles and her blouse was open. The 13 year-old girl believed the man had raped her.

When Leslie found out about this she had her daughter take a pregnancy test and she called a sexual assault crisis hotline for assistance. They advised her to report the incident to the police.

Leslie related to the officer that Darlene had been sexually assaulted about a year ago by the girl's biological father. That incident occurred while she visited him in Phoenix. The Phoenix Police Department investigated that assault and she had the report number. Leslie said that Darlene was severely traumatized over that incident with her father and she has been receiving counseling.

The deputy then completed his report and turned it in.

Findings of the El Mirage Police Review

This was obviously a very serious case that warranted immediate investigation by detectives. The 13 year-old victim was mentally retarded, vulnerable and suffering the trauma from a previous attack by her biological father.

A forensic interview of the victim should have been arranged to learn more specific details about the allegations she was making and a more detailed description of the suspect. If the examiner believed the allegations were true, then a rapist was still on the loose in El Mirage.

However, a review of this report revealed nothing beyond the responding deputy's initial report. The case had apparently been sent to the Maricopa County Sheriff's Special Victims Unit for follow up investigation by their detectives. But, there is no documentation that indicates they ever followed up on the case.

The El Mirage Police Department requested a complete copy of the Maricopa County Sheriff's Office investigation. Based on the police report the sheriff's office provided it appears that nothing more was ever done on this case.

The sheriff's report does not include any explanation as to why the case was not worked.

Sexual Assault by a Stranger

Sexual assault by a stranger is certainly the most traumatic of all assaults for a victim. It is an act of sexual violence in which the victim does not know their attacker.

"Serial rapists" are the most common sex offenders who attack women they do not know. They are motivated by a variety of dysfunctional conditions. Some of them act out aggression against women based on some deep psychological issues. Others are driven by low self-esteem and a need to prove their power and dominance over another person.

Many times the attacker will initially stalk a victim and study their lifestyle and daily patterns. Others are indiscriminate and will attack a woman based on an opportunity.

However, as the saying goes "opportunity does not *make* a rapist." A sex offender is *predisposed* to commit unlawful sexual acts and simply exploits the circumstances when presented with the opportunity.

Sexual Assault by an Acquaintance

This is the classification of sexual assault where the victim and offender knew each other. It is by far the most common type of sexual assault. Some studies conclude that nearly 85% of all reported sexual assaults are committed by someone known to the victim. On college or universities campuses that number is even higher.

It can be a first time encounter or date, or it could be someone the victim has known for a long time. It could be a neighbor, a co-worker, a casual or close friend, or even the victim's spouse or partner. (Most states now acknowledge spousal rape as a crime.) But, the bottom line is most of these assaults occur by someone the victim knew and trusted.

"Date rape" is a term used to describe a sexual assault that occurs between a couple who are involved in a "dating" relationship. The assault may occur on the first date or well into a prolonged relationship. The victim may be unwillingly, unwittingly or unknowingly coerced into sexual acts through the use of force, drugs or alcohol.

Spousal rape is probably the most underreported of all the sexual assaults. Due to family issues, perception barriers or even fear, many women never report sexual attacks by their husband or live-in boyfriend.

El Mirage Police Report

CASE # 06-1122101
Sexual Assault
April 12, 2006
Victim: 17 year-old female
Suspect: 18 year-old male

This case involves a 17 year-old girl who spent the night at a friend's house. Sometime during the night, her friend's 18 year-old brother came in her room and sexually assaulted her. The police were called to investigate.

Here is the police report:

Facts of the Case:

On April 12, 2006 at around 5:00 p.m. an El Mirage police officer was dispatched to the neighboring city of Youngtown, Arizona. A Youngtown police officer was at his station with a 17 year-old girl and her parents. The girl had just disclosed that she had been sexually assaulted by an 18 year-old man. The Youngtown officer determined that the assault occurred in the city of El Mirage and he called for the El Mirage officer to take over the case.

When the officer arrived he contacted the girl's parents "Thomas" and "Sheila" who told him they were at the Youngtown police station on an unrelated matter with their 17-year old daughter "Rosie." During some discussion with the police officer Rosie disclosed that she had been sexually assaulted.

Thomas said Rosie told them she had recently spent the night at her girlfriend "Jessie's" house in El Mirage. Rosie said that sometime during the night Jessie's older brother came in her room and sexually assaulted her. She said she didn't even know his name but knew he was 18 years-old.

Rosie said she was scared and didn't know what to do so she just "kept it inside" and didn't tell anybody until just now. Rosie's parents were very upset over what happened and said they wanted Jessie's brother prosecuted for what he did to their daughter.

The El Mirage officer said Rosie would need to be interviewed in detail about the assault. He told Rosie's parents that detectives would contact them and make the arrangements for a "forensic interview."

The officer asked the parents to get as much specific information about Jessie's brother as they could. He told them they especially needed his full name and address to move forward with the investigation.

Two days later Rosie's father called the El Mirage officer and gave him the name and address of Jessie's older brother who allegedly assaulted Rosie. The officer completed his report documenting all the information he was given. He requested the report be forwarded to the Special Victims Unit of the Maricopa County Sheriff's Office for follow up and to arrange for a forensic interview of the victim.

A supplemental report indicates this case was forwarded to the Special Victims Unit on May 17, 2006.

Findings of the El Mirage Police Review

This case includes a very serious allegation of sexual assault – one that could be reasonably solved and prosecuted. The victim claimed she was sexually assaulted in her friend's home. Her parents and family were very distressed over what happened to their daughter. The suspect is her friend's older brother and his identity is known. Clearly, this case warranted follow up investigation by the detectives.

The detectives should have arranged for a forensic interview of the victim. The use of a tape-recorded "confrontation call" between the victim and suspect may have been an effective strategy in this case if done in a timely manner.

However, based on the police report provided by the Maricopa County Sheriff's Office it appears this investigation was never completed. The police report indicates the Special Victims Unit was notified of the case, but there is no documentation explaining why they did not complete it.

Prevention

Sexual assault can happen anytime, anywhere and to anybody. While it is most commonly associated as a crime against women, men are sometimes sexually assaulted as well. Most of the sexual assaults described in the police reports in this chapter deal with female victims.

Women can minimize or reduce their chances of being victimized *by strangers* by taking certain precautions. They can avoid going out alone at night; stay away from dangerous or unfamiliar locations; keep their home or apartment secured; stay alert and aware of their surroundings - especially in isolated locations such as parking garages; learn personal defense techniques; and, lawfully acquire and learn to use a weapon.

Women can also take certain precautions to avoid sexual assaults by *acquaintances*. It is prudent to take whatever time is necessary to get to know a man before being alone with him. Women should insist on going to public places such as restaurants and movie theaters. And, they should avoid isolated locations until they feel comfortable with the person.

It is also a good idea to let a friend or family member know your whereabouts whenever you are out with an acquaintance. Don't hesitate to check in with them by cell phone to assure them you are OK. This will also send a message to your acquaintance that someone knows where you are and who you are with.

It is also advisable for a woman to remain in control of her mental faculties while on a date. They should not use drugs or alcohol in excess.

Women who date should become familiar with the concept of "date rape." They should be aware of the "tricks" that some sex offenders use to seduce or incapacitate their victims through the use of drugs and other means.

These suggestions are not meant to infer that women need to live in fear. Most of the men they meet are decent and will not harm them. Unfortunately, some dangers do exist and women have to be alert and take certain precautions to protect themselves.

Reporting Sexual Assault

Many women are initially reluctant to tell anyone they've been sexually assaulted. Some victims of sexual assault remain silent forever.

The decision to report a sexual assault is a difficult one for most victims. Quite often they simply want to push the ordeal from their psyche and move on with their life. Ultimately, the decision of whether to report the assault is up to the victim.

There are benefits associated with a sexual assault victim reporting the crime to the police. The victim will receive information about the entire process and will usually be teamed up with a "victim's advocate."

She will be given assistance from crisis intervention facilities or other treatment options. The victim will also receive information about questions she may have about sexually transmitted diseases and pregnancy.

The victim will also be kept informed about court proceedings and the on-going judicial process involved with the prosecution of her attacker.

El Mirage Police Report

CASE # 07-11221012
Sexual Assault
March 31, 2007
Victim: 12 year-old female
Suspect: 39 year-old male

This case involves a 12 year-old girl who was sexually assaulted by a 39 year-old convicted sex offender who also assaulted the girl's sister. The sexual assault was disclosed during a court proceeding and the Maricopa County Sheriff's Office was notified. The information was forwarded to the Special Victims Unit for investigation.

Here is the police report:

Facts of the Case:

On March 31, 2007 a Maricopa County Sheriff's deputy was contacted by a social worker from the Child Protective Services about a Sexual Assault that occurred near the 12700 block of West Dahlia Avenue in El Mirage. At that time the Maricopa County Sheriff's Office was under contract to provide police service to El Mirage.

The social worker "Ronnie" told the deputy that a 39 year-old convicted rapist "Steve" had sexually assaulted a 12 year-old girl named "Brittany" back in 2005 in El Mirage. The information about the sexual assault on Brittany was disclosed in open court on March 31, 2007 during Steve's sentencing for raping Brittany's sister. (He was sentenced to 35 years in prison on that charge.)

Ronnie provided the deputy with contact information for both Brittany and the suspect Steve. The deputy did not contact Brittany but confirmed the address where she was currently living in a group home in Glendale. The deputy completed an incident report and sent all the information to the Special Victims Unit for further investigation.

Findings of the El Mirage Police Review

Records indicate this case was assigned to the Special Victims Unit on April 5, 2007.

However, a review of this report revealed nothing was ever done on the case other than the deputy's initial incident report. While it might be true that the suspect was serving a long prison sentence for another rape, the 12 year-old victim in this case also deserved some justice.

The El Mirage Police Department requested a complete copy of the sheriff's report to see if the Special Victims Unit ever followed up on this case. There is no indication in those documents that they ever contacted or interviewed this victim.

In November 2007 an El Mirage police detective contacted the Deputy Maricopa County Attorney who prosecuted "Steve" for raping Brittany's sister. That attorney informed the detective that due to the length of Steve's prison sentence they would not file charges on Brittany's case.

So much for justice being served.

Preserving Evidence

If the woman chooses to report the attack to the police it is important that physical and forensic evidence be preserved. The victim should not shower or bathe until she has been examined by a doctor.

Victims should not wash or destroy the clothes they were wearing during the attack. It is important that the "crime scene" be left undisturbed and intact. Although difficult, victims should resist the urge to remove bodily fluids from clothing or wash bed linens.

To complete their investigation, the police will need a detailed description of the attacker. If at all possible the victim should be encouraged to write down or record all the pertinent details of the incident and a complete description of her attacker.

The victim should provide as much detail as possible to help the police identify, arrest and successfully prosecute her attacker. This process will also help the victim recall specific details of the traumatic event if she is later called to testify in court.

Psychologists believe that something as simple as writing down a description of the incident may help restore the victim's self-esteem. The healing process will begin as she actively participates in the police investigation.

The victim's direct involvement in the investigation may even give her a renewed sense of being in control over a situation in which she previously had no control.

As part of the police investigation, most victims of sexual assaults will be asked to undergo a medical examination to obtain forensic evidence. The exam is conducted by a trained doctor or nurse and is done in a medical facility or treatment center.

The evidence obtained through the examination is turned over to the police for scientific analysis at their crime lab. The evidence is then impounded and maintained for court purposes.

The police investigation will also require a series a photographs taken of the victim. The photos are normally taken by a police officer, detective or crime scene technician of the same gender as the victim. The police generally make every effort to ensure the victim's privacy and dignity are preserved regarding the photos.

Prosecution

Successful prosecution of sexual assault cases is not always simple. The victim will be asked to re-tell the details of her ordeal repeatedly. She may also have to describe the details of the attack to prosecuting and defense attorneys, and again in court.

The wheels of justice often turn slowly in our country. The prolonged waiting can be frustrating for some sexual assault victims. The preparation for trial of a sexual assault case can take many months. During the waiting period the victim could be asked to attend different court hearings, depositions and legal motions.

Many victims of sexual assault say their reluctance to report their attack is because of the intrusive and public nature of the criminal justice system. Publicly describing the details of her attack can cause a victim to feel self-conscious and embarrassed. Some fear the media exposure or the legal system itself. Many victims fear having to expose their personal life or sexual history during a trial.

But, Arizona and many other states have passed laws that protect sexual assault victims from such intrusions into their personal life while testifying in court. Many victims are unaware of that protection or simply do not trust the system. As a result, many sexual assaults go unreported and attackers are never brought to justice.

Some states also offer compensation to sexual assault victims who report their crimes. The victims may receive reimbursement or funding for medical expenses, examinations and counseling. Some state-funded programs even offer sexual assault victims compensation for lost wages.

Aside from a few tangible benefits, some sexual assault victims feel a sense of *empowerment* by participating in the prosecution of their attacker. Others say that it gives them strength to see their attacker face the consequences of his actions. Still others say it brings closure to a very traumatic event in their life.

Some say they feel an obligation to bring their attacker into court to face his crimes. They feel a sense of community obligation to prevent other women from being victimized by their attacker.

The benefits of women who prosecute their offenders are twofold. First, their participation helps to rid our society of rapists. Secondly, women who face their attackers in court help diminish the stigma of sexual assault victims testifying at trial.

El Mirage Police Report

CASE # 07-1050833
Sexual Assault
May 4, 2007
Victim: 16 year-old female
Suspect: 17 year-old male

This case involves a 16 year-old girl who was visiting some friends at a home in El Mirage. A 17 year-old male acquaintance slipped a drug into the girl's drink and incapacitated her. The male then sexually assaulted the girl. A Maricopa County Sheriff's deputy was dispatched to investigate.

Here is the police report:

Facts of the Case:

On May 9, 2007 around 7:15 p.m. a Maricopa County Sheriff's deputy received a message from his dispatcher to contact a man named "Billy." The dispatcher told him that Billy wanted to report that his younger sister had been sexually assaulted in a home in El Mirage. The Maricopa County Sheriff's Office was under contract to provide police service to El Mirage so a sheriff's deputy was summoned to do the investigation.

The deputy called Billy to get the details about what occurred. Billy told the deputy he was 25 years old. He said his 16 year-old sister Alice told him she had been sexually assaulted by a guy she knew named "Daniel." Alice said Daniel slipped something into her drink and then sexually assaulted her.

The incident occurred while Alice was visiting at the home of Daniel's mother on Aster Drive in El Mirage. Alice said she woke up during the incident and found Daniel having sexual intercourse with her. She told him to "stop" but he refused and continued assaulting her.

Billy said Alice told their mother what happened but the mother was reluctant to believe Alice's story. He explained that their mother works for the State of Arizona on behalf of sex offenders.

The deputy told Billy that he would come to their home to get more information about the incident.

When the deputy arrived at the home he spoke with Billy and Alice's mother "Ruth." Ruth told the deputy she was aware of the incident and believed it had occurred a few days earlier on Monday. The deputy asked why the incident hadn't been brought to the attention of the police earlier.

Ruth said she wanted to get "the truth" before it was brought to the attention of the police. She said she works with sex offenders and realizes that Daniel would have to register as a sex offender for the rest of his life over this incident. Ruth said she didn't want to "ruin Daniel's life" if her daughter's allegation was untrue.

The deputy did not speak directly to Alice about the incident but she was standing outside talking with her brother. At one point Alice overheard the conversation between the deputy and her mother. Alice yelled out, "mom he raped me!"

The deputy informed both Alice and Ruth that he would be forwarding his report to the Special Victims Unit and detectives would be in contact with them.

At that point the deputy completed his initial report on the Sexual Assault. He turned the report into his supervisor and it was forwarded to the Special Victims Unit.

Findings of the El Mirage Police Review

This was a case that clearly had several workable leads and could have been solved by detectives. A 16 year-old girl had been slipped some drugs and was sexually assaulted by an acquaintance.

Detectives should have arranged for an in-depth interview of the victim to determine whether she was telling the truth. Because the suspect's identity was known, the detectives could have attempted a "confrontation call" between the victim and the suspect. At the very least, the detectives should have picked up the suspect for questioning about the alleged sexual assault.

However, the report indicates that nothing more was done with this investigation by the Special Victims Unit. There is no information in the Maricopa County Sheriff's report that explains why the case was not completed.

Treatment

Regardless of whether a victim reports a sexual assault there are still treatment facilities and support programs available to them. Many communities provide sexual assault counselors and victim advocate programs through their police or prosecuting agencies.

Many states, including Arizona, have spent years re-developing their protocols for handling sexual assaults. From the initial police response to interview techniques to crisis counseling, authorities now employ consistent and sensitive methods of dealing with the needs of sexual assault victims. These new approaches have all been developed with the assistance of victim advocate organizations to help minimize the negative impact of sexual assaults.

Many law enforcement agencies, states' attorneys and prosecutors have implemented victim advocate programs to work directly with victims of sexual assault. Many provide professional counselors to assist victims with the emotional trauma of their ordeal. Most agencies assign an advocate to keep the victim informed of hearings, plea agreements and trial dates throughout the process of prosecuting their offender. Some programs also assist the victims in obtaining compensation or restitution.

Effects Of Sexual Assault

Most sexual assault victims say they feared they would be *seriously* injured during the assault. This is usually a result of threats and force used by their attacker.

However, only a *very* small percentage of sexual assaults result in *serious* physical injury to the victims; such attacks are very rare. They are typically committed by a stranger and can be extremely violent.

Nearly two-thirds of all sexual assault victims do not suffer any *physical* injuries at all. And those victims who *are* injured suffer only minor physical injuries such as cuts, bruises, or trauma to their genitals.

While most sexual assault victims suffer no *physical* injury, the *psychological* and *emotional* trauma to the victims can be devastating.

Many victims of sexual assault will suffer a variety of emotional effects. They can experience anxiety, depression, nightmares, insomnia, anger, guilt and shame.

Another real danger for the victim of sexual assault is being inflicted with a sexually transmitted disease (STD). This can have a paralyzing effect on the victim if the disease is incurable or the victim is married.

Victims of sexual assault react in a variety of different manners. Some will experience a loss of interest in sex; others may become socially withdrawn; some may display hyper-vigilance (extreme fear); others may even contemplate suicide.

Some women develop *serious* emotional disorders as a result of sexual assault. Those victims require professional psychological help to recover from their experience. This is most common in cases of a violent sexual assault by a stranger.

At least one sexual assault treatment center for women describes a syndrome as Sexual Assault-related Post Traumatic Stress Disorder (PTSD). They conclude that one-third of all sexual assault victims suffer from this disorder sometime during their life.

(The term PTSD was institutionalized during the Vietnam War to describe a clinical diagnosis characterized by flashbacks, depression and outbursts of rage by soldiers returning from combat. During previous wars, a similar disorder among combat soldiers was commonly referred to as "combat fatigue.")

Following a sexual assault, a woman may be diagnosed with PTSD when the psychological and physiological effects from the assault impair her ability to function in family, work or social settings.

El Mirage Police Report

CASE # 06-1050804
Sexual Assault
August 13, 2006
Victim: 12-year old female
Suspect: 18-year old male

This case involves a 12 year-old girl who accepted a ride home from an 18 year-old schoolmate. During the ride home the 18 year-old man sexually abused the young girl. The police were called to investigate.

Here is the police report:

Facts of the Case:

On August 13, 2006 a uniformed El Mirage Police patrol officer was dispatched to a home on north 140th Drive in the neighboring city of Surprise, Arizona. The call was in reference to a possible Sexual Assault that occurred at a school in the city of El Mirage.

When the El Mirage officer arrived at the residence he was contacted by a Surprise Police officer who told him that the family was reporting the sexual assault of their 12-year old daughter "Jessica." While questioning the family the Surprise officer determined that the offense had actually occurred in El Mirage's jurisdiction. At that point the El Mirage officer took over the investigation.

The El Mirage officer conducted a tape-recorded interview of 12 year-old Jessica's parents. The parents relayed to the officer what their daughter told them had occurred.

Jessica told her parents that when school let out on July 12, 2006 she received a ride home from an 18 year-old classmate from her school named "John." Although she is only 12 years old and he is 18 years old, both Jessica and John are in the same class.

According to her mother Jessica told her that while driving her home 18 year-old John touched Jessica's breast on the outside of her clothing. She told her parents that John then asked her, "What do I get for this ride home?" Jessica asked John what he meant and he told her he wanted either "oral sex or regular sex." Jessica said she told John "no."

The girl also told her parents that another incident occurred sometime between July 12, 2006 and August 11, 2006 involving the same 18 year-old male student. Jessica said that time an incident occurred inside the classroom at school. She said that John put his hand up her skirt touching her leg. Jessica told her parents that John took her hand and pushed it down his pants. Jessica said that when John did that she "separated herself" from him and moved to another location.

The girl's mother went on to tell the police officer that she had received a phone call from Jessica's school nurse two days earlier on August 11, 2006. The nurse asked whether Jessica was able to receive Tylenol for a headache. The nurse went on to say that there had been an altercation at the school between her daughter and an 18-year old male student (John). Apparently, the altercation started when the John found out that Jessica had told a female friend about what had occurred in the car when John had driven her home. Upon hearing what had happened to their daughter the parents called the police.

The first-responder El Mirage police officer completed a police report entitled Sexual Assault. In the report he documented what Jessica told her parents had occurred and the identity of the 18 year-old John.

A police supervisor later reviewed the police report. The supervisor wrote a supplemental report stating that "due to the nature of the allegations being Sexual Assault, this report will be forwarded to the Maricopa County Sheriff's Office Special Victims Unit for follow-up."

Findings of the El Mirage Police Review

The allegations brought forth by the victim in this case are very disturbing. A 12 year-old girl had been victimized by an adult schoolmate on more than one occasion. The young girl was experiencing physiological and emotional issues from the incidents. Detectives should have followed up on this case.

The detectives should have immediately notified the school about the allegations involving their students. While the investigation was on-going precautions should have been taken to protect other female students from the alleged offender.

Detectives should have arranged for a "forensic interview" of the victim. The suspect's identity was known and they should have looked into his background. At the very least, the 18-year old suspect should have been picked up for questioning.

The report indicates the Special Victims Unit was notified about this case. However, there is no documentation in the report that indicates they ever completed the investigation. From all indications nothing more was ever done on this case.

Helping A Sexual Assault Victim

Immediately after a woman is sexually assaulted it is important that she is taken to an environment where she feels safe and secure. She may feel emotionally shattered; her dignity and privacy must be safeguarded. If the victim suffered physical injuries it is important she receives immediate medical treatment from paramedics or at a hospital.

The effects of sexual assault can be very traumatic and may require long-term counseling. Even victims who decide not to publicly report their attack may need guidance and comfort from talking with a close friend or family member.

Professional help is always the best suggestion for sexual assault victims. People trained in victim advocacy are best suited to guide the victim towards the road to recovery. Most major cities have sexual assault hotlines and treatment centers available to assist victims.

But, sexual assault victims mostly need understanding and caring from friends and family members. They need the company of those they can trust. Most of them feel personally violated and their trust betrayed.

Victims of sexual assault will react in different manners. Child victims will likely respond differently than adults; victims of violent sexual assault by a stranger will likely react differently than a victim of an assault by an acquaintance. But, the pain and humiliation each has suffered are the same.

The level of violence used by the attacker and the severity of the attack will also have an impact on the victim. The extent of the victim's injuries or disfigurement may also play a role.

Some victims of sexual assault recover quickly and others may suffer the effects of the attack for their entire lives. A victim's age, level of life experience and maturity will impact their ability to deal with sexual assault. The manner in which a victim is treated by first-responders (police officers and paramedics) can also affect a victim's recovery.

Married women who have been sexually assaulted by a stranger or even an acquaintance can endure additional problems. The relationship with their spouse could be affected by the assault. The maturity level of the victim's spouse, how they react, and the manner in which they treat the victim, will all play a significant role in her recovery.

The Healing Process

Sexual assault is a devastating crime. It not only affects the victim but it can also impact the victim's loved ones as well. Close friends and family of the victim not only have to deal with the care and recovery of the victim but they also have to deal with their own anger and other emotions they may feel from the victim's ordeal.

Provide comfort to the victim and let her know she is not alone in dealing with her attack. Show compassion and understanding by being a good listener and not judging the victim. Help her through the feelings of shame and guilt and convince her that the assault was not her fault. Provide reassurance that the victim is loved and cared for.

It is important to remember that a victim of sexual assault has been forced into acts against their will. The ordeal has likely stripped them of their self-esteem and they need reassurance.

Sexual assault victims may not be thinking clearly and may simply be looking for comfort from a trusting friend or family member. Do not pass blame or judgment on the victim. Their self-esteem is most likely in jeopardy and they are in need of reassurance and caring. Talk to the person with understanding and compassion.

Discuss the victim's different options and encourage her to report the attack. Encourage the victim to obtain a medical evaluation and treatment. If necessary, assist the victim in obtaining professional counseling or treatment. But, allow the victim to make her own decisions. Offer advice and suggestions and describe the options that are available but allow her make the ultimate decision.

About half of all sexual assault victims never report the crime. Many women suffer the consequences in silence and their attackers go undetected and are free to sexually assault others. It is a vicious cycle that has to change.

Sexual assault is one of the most underreported violent crimes in our country.

Today we have a better understanding of the implications and consequences of sexual assault. It is a personal experience that violates the human body and can leave physical and emotional scars on the victim.

The manner in which authorities handle sexual assaults has improved drastically over the past 20 years. Widespread reforms in favor of the victim's rights have made the process less intrusive for women who have been sexually assaulted. A complex criminal justice system has given way to a better understanding of the impact of sexual assaults.

****

Chapter 13

Other Sex Crimes Against Children

Chapter 13 examines the details of five police reports that were mishandled by the Maricopa County Sheriff's Office. The victims of these cases were children who were sexually exploited by an adult, sexually abused or molested.

This chapter also includes statistical and anecdotal information about these crimes and the effects they can have on victims. It also provides parents with suggestions and advice on ways to protect their children from sexual abuse.

El Mirage Police Report

CASE # 07-1050836
Sexual Misconduct With a Minor
Date: May 28, 2007
Victim: 15 year-old female
Suspect: 21 year-old male

This case involves a 15 year-old girl who was involved in a consensual sexual relationship with a 21 year-old man. A dispute occurred between the girl's family and the man. The police were called to investigate.

Here is the police report:

Facts of the Case:

On May 28, 2007 around 9:15 p.m. a Maricopa County Sheriff's deputy responded to a home near El Mirage and Thunderbird Roads in El Mirage on a call of a Civil Matter. The Maricopa County Sheriff's Office was under contract to provide police service to El Mirage so a sheriff's deputy was summoned to handle the call.

When the deputy arrived he made contact with "Phillip" who told the deputy he placed the call to the police. He told the deputy that he had been living with his girlfriend's family in their home near 122nd Ave. & Valentine Ave. Phillip said that about 30 minutes earlier he had gotten into a verbal argument with his girlfriend's parents "Thomas" and "Valerie." The argument was over some yard work they wanted him to do at a neighbor's house.

Phillip told the deputy that Valerie told him he could no longer stay at the house and he needed to remove his belongings. He said he started packing his clothes but the arguing escalated. Phillip said that's when Thomas got involved.

Phillip said that Thomas made a fist and came at him in an aggressive manner so he swung back in "self defense." He thought he might have struck Thomas in the head. At that point Thomas chased Phillip from the house and told him to stay away. Phillip said he ran to a friend's house on El Mirage Road and called the police.

Phillip said he wanted the deputy to stand by while he removed his belongings from the house. The deputy told him he would go to the house and speak with Valerie to see if it was OK for him to remove his belongings.

The deputy went to the address on Valentine Ave. and contacted Valerie to find out what happened. Valerie immediately made allegations that Phillip, who is 21 years old, made threats to "rape" her 15 year-old daughter "Kendra." Valerie further alleged that Phillip had been having sex with Kendra. Valerie demanded that charges be filed against Phillip for having sex with a minor.

The deputy asked Valerie to explain what she meant about Phillip threatening to "rape" Kendra. Valerie explained that while she and Phillip were arguing, Kendra also started arguing with Phillip. Valerie told the deputy that while Phillip was walking up the stairs to get his belongings she heard him say to Kendra, "You're lucky I don't rape you right now."

The deputy also asked Valerie what the relationship was between Phillip and Kendra. She told the deputy that the two had engaged in sexual activity "about five times."

Valerie said she became aware that Phillip and Kendra were having sex about two months ago. The deputy asked her why she didn't call the police at that time. Valerie said she did call but the operator told her they would not dispatch an officer because "she did not have any proof." The deputy said that he found that hard to believe and asked if she knew the name of the operator she spoke to. Valerie said she did not know the operator's name.

The deputy asked Valerie how Phillip, a 21 year-old man ended up living in her home and dating her 15 year-old daughter. Valerie said that Kendra met Phillip on a "chat line" and they became friends.

At that point the deputy spoke briefly to Kendra about her relationship with Phillip. The deputy asked Kendra if she ever had sex with Phillip and where it occurred. She told the deputy that she and Phillip had sex five times inside her home.

The deputy asked Kendra if the sex was consensual and Kendra said only two of the times were consensual. When the deputy asked her about the non-consensual sex Kendra seemed uncomfortable answering that in front of her mother. The deputy did not pursue that line of questioning at that point. Kendra did confirm that she met Phillip on a "chat line."

At that point the deputy re-contacted Phillip to question him further about his relationship with Kendra. He told the deputy he first met Kendra on a "chat line" about five months ago at which time she told him she was 18 years old. After talking on the phone for a few weeks he and Valerie decided they wanted to meet in person. He was working at a McDonald's in Phoenix at the time and Kendra's mother drove her to the McDonald's so they could meet.

Phillip said he was living alone in an apartment in Phoenix at the time. He and Kendra soon became fond of each other and Kendra eventually asked him to move into her home in El Mirage which he did.

The deputy asked Phillip if he ever had sex with Kendra and he said "yes." He said that he found out she was only 15 years old about two months after they started having sex. Phillip acknowledged that he kept having sex with Kendra after he learned she was only 15 years old.

Phillip said that Kendra's mother was aware they were having sex and she was "OK with it." Phillip denied the allegation of threatening to "rape" Kendra and only admitted to consensual sex.

The deputy obtained Phillips identification and asked where he was planning to live. He said he would be staying with his friend on El Mirage Road for a while.

The deputy notified a supervisor about the situation and completed his initial police report. The case was then forwarded to the Maricopa County Sheriff's Office Special Victims Unit for further investigation.

Findings of the El Mirage Police Review

This case warranted further investigation. The 21 year-old suspect admitted he continued to engage in consensual sexual intercourse with the 15 year-old girl even after he found out her true age. That constitutes a felony criminal act of Sexual Misconduct with a Minor. The issue of non-consensual sex raised by the victim still needed to be resolved. Detectives also needed to arrange for a forensic interview of the victim.

While it appears this was clearly a prosecutable case, nothing in the report indicates the Special Victims Unit did any follow up work on this investigation. There is no documentation that the investigation was ever completed. Furthermore, there is no information in the Maricopa County Sheriff's report that explains why this case was not completed by their Special Victims Unit.

Sexual Misconduct with Minors

In Arizona, the crime of Sexual Misconduct with a Minor (A.R.S.13-1405) is designed to protect children and young teens from sexual exploitation by adults. A young girl's willingness or consent to engage in sex with an adult is irrelevant.

Sexual Misconduct with a Minor is a very serious offense – a felony. If convicted of this offense the adult will be a required to register as a Sex Offender for the rest his life.

The Law

In most states it is a felony to engage in sexual acts with a person under the age of 18 years. In Arizona for example, if the minor is 15-17 years of age it is a *Class 6 Felony* punishable by up to two years in prison.

Sexual Misconduct with a Minor in which the victim was 14 years-old or younger is a *Class 2 Felony.* If convicted of just a single count of this crime, the person could be sentenced up to 27 years in prison – depending on certain mandatory sentencing criteria (*Dangerous Crimes Against Children* statute).

As described earlier in this chapter, the crime of Sexual Assault is committing sexual acts *without* the victim's consent. The difference between the crime of Sexual Misconduct with a Minor and Sexual Assault is usually the element of *consent*.

A 14 year-old girl may "consent" to have sex with a 22 year-old man, but it is *still* a violation of this statute. Under this law, the girl is considered a victim of this crime and the man would be charged with a Class 2 Felony.

Many states have separate sets of laws for adults and juveniles – both as victims *and* offenders. The criminal justice system handles juvenile offenders differently than adults. This is based on the premise that juveniles are not fully matured and should be afforded greater leniency for committing offenses.

In Arizona, a person under the age of 18 years will be adjudicated in Juvenile Court for a criminal charge unless they have been "remanded" by a judge to stand trial in an adult court.

Likewise, certain laws specifically protect juveniles who have been *victimized* – especially sex crimes. Again, these laws are based on the assumption that juveniles are not mature enough to make informed decisions about sex.

The penalties for violations of these laws are protracted to be even more severe for victimizing younger children. As described above, the penalties are quite severe for an adult who engages in sex with a 14 year-old girl; however, the penalties are less severe if the girl is 16 or 17 years old.

A Possible Defense

Depending on the circumstances, an adult charged with Sexual Misconduct with a Minor could have a possible criminal "defense" under the law. If the accused man *"reasonably believed"* the underage girl was actually 18 years or older he could present that as a defense. For example, if the girl *told* him she was 18 years old *and* she looked older than 17 then the man might have a legitimate defense.

However, the "age" defense would no longer be a viable option if the man subsequently learned the underage girl's *real* age and continued to engage in sex with her.

El Mirage Police Report

CASE # 06-1050805
Child Molesting
February 24, 2006
Victim: Female girls 12-years old and younger
Suspect/s: Older teenage girls in a group home

This case involves a situation where a 15 year-old girl who lived in a state-run foster-care "group home." During a session with her therapist she disclosed that some of the older girls in the facility were engaging in sexual activity with some of the younger girls. The police were called to investigate.

(Special note: The 15-year old complainant later recanted all allegations.)

Here is the police report:

Facts of the Case:

On February 24, 2006 a female El Mirage police officer received a telephone call from a psychiatrist who reported that one his patients, 15-year old "Annie," told him that "sexual activity" was occurring between some of the girls in the "group home" in El Mirage where she resides. The home was a state-licensed facility.

The doctor also told the officer that Annie said there are photographs inside the group home depicting some of the sexual activity. Specifically, Annie told the doctor that there is a photo in her own dresser drawer that depicts the sexual activity.

The psychiatrist told the El Mirage officer that Annie related to him she had been trying to get out of the group home. She said that "17-year old girls were doing sexual things with 12-year old girls." Apparently, Annie told the doctor that she was not involved in any of the sexual activity.

The El Mirage officer asked the doctor if Annie had indicated whether any of the care-givers or staff members of the group home were involved in the sexual activity. He told the officer that she had not mentioned that. But, Annie did say that she is disliked by the staff of the group home and whenever she tries to report activity no one believes her. The officer concluded her phone conversation with the psychiatrist and informed her sergeant about the allegations at the group home.

The female officer reported that she has had many interactions with Annie during her duties as an El Mirage officer. She thought that it was odd that Annie had never mentioned anything in her past contacts with her about the alleged sexual activity in the group home. The officer also reported that she had been in the group home several times while on-duty, including in Annie's room, and had never seen any photos or anything else in plain view that might suggest sexual activity.

The initial police report entitled Child Molesting was completed and turned into a sergeant. According to police records this case was then assigned to the Maricopa County Sheriff's Office Special Victims Unit for follow up investigation.

Findings of the El Mirage Police Review

According to the report, the Maricopa County Sheriff's Office Special Victims Unit was initially assigned this case for follow up investigation in February 2006. It appears that the sheriff's office did not complete this case and it was returned to El Mirage in 2007.

In 2008 a detective with the El Mirage Police Department located and contacted the Director of the former group home. The detective told her he was looking into the allegation that Annie had made in April 2006. The former group home director explained that she had been made aware of the allegations back in 2006. She believed that the Arizona Child Protective Services had investigated the matter and found the allegations to be false. According to the director, Annie had later recanted her allegations to her therapist and to her social worker.

The director told the detective that the home had been licensed by the State of Arizona and authorized to care for children in the care of the Arizona Child Protective Services. It was later closed down in September 2006.

There is no record or documentation that indicates that the Special Victims Unit did any work on this case. Furthermore, there is nothing in their report to indicate the sheriff's office even knew the 15-year old girl had recanted her story. That information was developed by an El Mirage detective and documented in a police report some 2½ years after the girl first made the allegations.

If these allegations of young girls being sexually molested in a state-sanctioned foster home had been legitimate, the fallout from this case would have likely had far reaching consequences.

Fortunately, in the end this case involved only false allegations – or so it would appear.

Child Sex Crimes

Sexual crimes against children can be a difficult or even distasteful topic for some people to discuss. But, like it or not, sexual abuse and sexual misconduct with minors occurs every day in this country.

The subject of sex crimes against children has been widely studied, has countless advocacy programs and has been the focus of most state legislatures for the past 10 years. Law enforcement officers and others who are in the business of protecting children generally concur that sexual abuse of children is quite common and poses a serious problem in our society

However, it is often difficult for researchers to gather reliable statistics about the sexual abuse of children. One of the problems is underreporting. Researchers believe that boys have a greater tendency to *not* disclose their victimization. And statistically, girls are sexually abused far more often than boys.

Children of every race and economic status may become victims of sexual abuse. Sexual abuse of children can happen in many different environments. Parents often try their best to protect their children from sexual abusers but it sometimes proves a difficult task.

Effects on the Child

As described in previous chapters the effects of sexual abuse on a child range from very little to deep emotional trauma. Many younger children are resilient and respond well to counseling and other treatment.

Children who suffered more severe or prolonged sexual abuse may react with a higher degree of behavioral problems. These victims may display depression, fear, and outbursts of anger. Child victims of long-term sexual abuse may suffer sexual dysfunctions as an adult.

However, most young children who have been sexually molested or abused on a single occasion are likely to fully recover with no long-term issues.

Regardless of the circumstances parents are advised to seek professional help for any child victim of sexual abuse.

El Mirage Police Report

CASE # 07-1122107
Child Molesting
June 23, 2007
Victim: 5 year-old female
Suspect: 13 year-old male

This case involves a 5 year-old girl whose parents asked a neighbor family to babysit her while they went to the movies. The young girl later disclosed to her parents that she was left alone with the babysitting family's 13 year-old son and he sexually abused her. The police were called to investigate.

Here is the police report:

Facts of the Case:

On June 23, 2007 around 11:00 a.m. an El Mirage police officer responded to a residence in the 12000 block of Boca Raton Avenue in El Mirage on a call of a Child Molesting.

When the officer arrived he contacted the victim's parents "Rodney" and "Melanie." Rodney told the officer that last night he and his wife had plans to go out. The neighbors across the street "Cathy" and "John" agreed to babysit their 5 year-old daughter "Katie."

Around 6:30 p.m. they dropped Katie off with Cathy and John before they went out. Cathy and John's 13 year-old son "Brad" was also at the house.

Melanie told the officer they picked up Katie about two hours later around 8:30 p.m. When they got home Katie told her parents she and Brad had watched the movie "High School Musical" in Brad's room. She also disclosed to her parents that Brad had touched her inappropriately.

Katie explained to her parents that Brad lifted up her dress and put his hand underneath her panties. The 5 year-old girl told her parents Brad "touched her vagina." Katie then patted her own vagina area (with her clothes on) to demonstrate where Brad touched her.

The officer asked Katie if she wanted to talk to him about what happened but the little girl just kept hiding from the officer. As the officer was talking to Katie's parents, she leaned over to her father and said in a soft voice, "tell him about Brad." The comment was unsolicited by the officer or the little girl's parents.

Rodney said he and his wife decided to confront their neighbors about what happened. The next morning they went to Cathy and John's home and told them what Katie said Brad did to her. Cathy did acknowledge that Katie and Brad had been alone in Brad's room last night watching the movie.

Randy and Melanie said they later heard Cathy yelling at Brad saying, "did you hear what they said you did?" They heard Brad respond, "I didn't do it, I didn't do it."

Cathy told Rodney and Melanie they would get Brad, "counseling or something."

Rodney and Melanie said they were "in shock" and very upset over what had happened to their daughter. They discussed it and decided to report the incident to the police. Both parents said they wanted the incident investigated and would aid in prosecution.

The officer then notified his supervisor of the situation. The sergeant then notified the Special Victims Unit of the Maricopa County Sheriff's Office. The officer completed his report and turned it in to his sergeant.

The officer's report indicates it was being forwarded to the Special Victims Unit for follow up investigation by detectives.

Findings of the El Mirage Police Review

The victim's parents wanted the case investigated and agreed to cooperate. The 5 year-old girl's allegation seemed plausible. Young girls of that age typically don't make specific allegations of that nature unless they are true. Nonetheless, a forensic interview of the victim should have been arranged to learn more specific details about the allegations she was making. If the examiner believed the allegations were true, then detectives should have attempted to interview the 13 year-old neighbor boy.

However, a review of this report revealed nothing beyond the responding officer's initial report. The El Mirage Police Department requested a complete copy of the sheriff's investigation to see if the Special Victims Unit ever followed up on the case. Based on the police report they gave to El Mirage it appears that nothing more was ever done on this investigation. The sheriff's report does not include any explanation as to why the case was not completed.

Babysitters

For most parents finding a reliable babysitter is often a problem. Many parents are willing to spend extra money for the peace of mind that comes with a reputable and experienced babysitter.

Sometimes parents will ask for childcare assistance from a friend or acquaintance. They may feel comfortable because their friend has children of their own and may appear to be well-adjusted.

But, even babysitters that appear to be reputable and dependable can result in a nightmare situation for both the parents and child. Hidden dangers may exist and some are not easy to detect. It is advisable to ask for references, determine their level of experience and even question their knowledge of first aid and life saving.

It is also advisable for parents to ask other questions or otherwise determine the family's home environment. Who else lives in the house? What are their gender and ages? Are there any physical barriers or dangers such as a swimming pool, aggressive pets? What is the alcohol use in the home? The decision to leave your child might very well be based on the answers to these questions.

El Mirage Police Report

CASE # 07-11221011
Sexual Abuse, Assault
March 30, 2007
Victim: 15 year-old female
Suspect: 20 year-old male

This case involves a 15 year-old girl and her younger sister who were playing in a neighborhood park. The girls were approached by an adult male who began talking with them. The man pulled the older girl close to him and sexually abused her. Both girls ran home and their parents called the police to investigate.

Here is the police report:

Facts of the Case:

On March 30, 2007 around 5:40 p.m. an El Mirage officer responded to a residence in the 12100 block of West Shaw Butte Avenue in reference to suspicious activity that just occurred in a nearby community park.

When the officer arrived he contacted "Susan" who said she had called the police. Also there was Susan's 15 year-old daughter "Kristi."

Susan gave the officer a brief overview of what had happened but she said her daughter could provide more details. The officer then asked Kristi what happened.

Kristi said she had taken her little sister to a nearby community park to play around 4:45 p.m. She said there was a Hispanic man in the park who approached them. Kristi said the guy seemed nice and asked her how old she was. She said she told the man she was 15 years old and he told her he was 20 years old. She said they started talking about high school and music.

Kristi told the officer the man then reached out and asked to shake her hand. She thought he was just being nice and put her hand out. Kristi said the guy then pulled her towards him and kissed her on the cheek.

They started talking more about music and the guy asked for another handshake. This time he grabbed her hand and pulled her close to him and told her she was cute.

Kristi said he wouldn't let go of her hand and pulled her harder towards him and grabbed her buttocks. She said he then reached up and grabbed her right breast and fondled it while telling her she had "beautiful eyes." Kristi said she told the man "Get the fuck away from me" and pulled away from his grasp. She said she grabbed her little sister and ran home.

The officer asked her for a description of the guy and she said he was a Hispanic man, around 20 years old with short black hair. She said he was wearing a black tee-shirt and light colored blue jeans. Kristi said the guy was wearing sunglasses on top of his head.

The officer asked if the man was still in the park. Kristi said he was still there when she left. Susan said her husband "Rick" had gone back to the park with Kristi and she pointed out the man to him.

Apparently, Rick then took Kristi home and then followed the guy as he walked along Cactus Road. Rick called his wife and told her he followed the guy to a house on N. 121st Lane and it appeared the guy lived there. The house was only two blocks away from their home. Rick told her he saw the man get into a green car at that address and then drive away. The car appeared to be a green Mitsubishi with front-end damage. Rick tried to follow him but lost him in the residential area.

The officer asked Susan if they wished to follow through with charges against the man for inappropriately touching their daughter. She said they did and would assist in prosecution. Kristi said she could identify the guy if she saw him again.

When Kristi's dad arrived back at home the officer got the address to where he had followed the suspect. The officer drove to that house to find out who lived there.

The officer knocked on the door and contacted a Hispanic male who identified himself as "Juan." Juan did not match the description of the man Kristi had described.

Through talking to Juan the officer was able to determine the man who lived at that house was "Antonio." Juan told the officer Antonio owned a green Mitsubishi with front end damage and had driven away from house a few minutes earlier.

Juan said he did not know where Antonio went. The officer asked if he knew what Antonio was wearing. Juan told him he was wearing a black tee-shirt and jeans. The officer asked if Antonio was wearing sunglasses and he said "yes."

The officer attempted to locate Antonio but was unsuccessful. He completed his report and notified his supervisor about the incident. The officer's report indicates he faxed a copy of the report to the sergeant at the Special Victims Unit.

Findings of the El Mirage Police Review

This was a case that clearly warranted follow up by the detectives. The officer's initial report included enough information to track down and arrest the suspect. It appeared that the suspect lived only two blocks from the victim which was disconcerting to their family.

The officer's initial report indicates he faxed the case over to the sergeant in charge of the Special Victims Unit at the Maricopa County Sheriff's Office.

However, a review of this report revealed nothing was ever done on the case beyond the responding officer's initial report. There is no documentation that shows the investigation was ever completed.

Child Safety

Parents have a responsibility to teach their children how to be safe. They coach their children about dangerous items around the house and the importance of wearing seatbelts in the car. As children get older parents also have a responsibility to teach their children about the real-world dangers of sexual abuse and sexual predators.

It is often a delicate balance between trusting people and being cautious. Explaining where the lines are between appropriate and inappropriate physical contact can be difficult. Police officers will always warn parents to err on the side of caution when it comes to their children and strangers.

As adults we know that real dangers lurk in the real world. We generally know how to recognize a dangerous situation or environment.

But, our children are born to innocence which makes them vulnerable. They may not be as quick to sense a dangerous situation as an adult. And, unfortunately, there are adults who exploit the vulnerability and innocence of children.

Teach Your Children

Effective parenting means teaching your child how to react when they find themselves in a troubling situation. It also means demonstrating how to use the phone to call

9-1-1 in an emergency. Responsible parents also talk with the children about *running away* from uncomfortable or dangerous situations and how to seek shelter.

Parents should never overreact to their child's disclosure of an unpleasant encounter. Children will emulate their parents as a role model. They must feel confident that they can tell their parents *anything*.

Children respond well to play-acting. Talk with your children about real-life dangers. Then follow up that conversation by playing out "scenarios" with them to see how they respond. Remember, children need age-appropriate, positive reinforcement to feel confident in themselves.

Parents can use drive-time in the car with their children to discuss "what-if" situations. If a child is exposed to a TV news story about another child who has been victimized, the parent could ask their child how they would have responded or reacted in that situation.

It is impossible to protect our children from every danger in the world. We can, however, prepare them to react properly to many situations to keep them safe and out of harm's way.

El Mirage Police Report

CASE # 06-1050820
Sexual Abuse
June 10. 2006
Victim: 5 year-old male
Suspect: 10 year-old male

This case involves a 5 year-old boy whose family found out he had been coerced into engaging in oral sexual activity with his 10 year-old cousin. The police were called to investigate.

Here is the police report:

Facts of the Case:

On June 10, 2006 an El Mirage police officer received a call from a child psychologist named "Dr. Padilla." The doctor informed the officer that he had a family visit him at his counseling office in Phoenix. He said the father "Raul" had learned that his 5 year-old son "Nino" had been engaging in oral sexual activity with his 10 year-old cousin "Alberto."

Dr. Padilla was told that Alberto lives on 131st Lane in El Mirage and Nino often visits at that location. Apparently, the sex acts have occurred on multiple occasions in different parts of the house including in the garage, laundry room and at the side of the house.

The officer asked the doctor if he had any more specific information about the sexual activity. The doctor told the officer he was unsure as to who did what, but Nino also told his parents that Alberto had "gotten behind him." The parents were concerned that Alberto may have tried or had anal sex with their 5 year-old son.

Dr. Padilla told the officer he had not interviewed Nino.

The officer asked the doctor why the family didn't report the incident to the police prior to disclosing it to him. Dr. Padilla said that the family was unclear about what to do and assumed their insurance provider was going to contact the police.

The doctor provided the officer with the contact information for the family who lives in Mesa, Arizona.

The officer made several attempts to contact the family via telephone leaving several messages. He also contacted Child Protective Services and briefed them on what he had learned thus far. The agent took down the information and assigned a case number.

On June 18, 2006 the 5 year-old boy's father Raul called the El Mirage officer.

The officer asked Raul how he learned about the incident between his son Nino and his nephew Alberto. He said that recently he saw Nino playing with a neighbor boy in their yard. Raul said he saw Nino guiding the other boy's head toward his crotch area. The father told the officer he became alarmed at seeing this behavior and asked Nino about it.

The 5 year-old boy told his father that's how he and his cousin Alberto "played." Nino told his father that Alberto has him "suck his dick." According to Raul, his son referred to this as "playing mommy and daddy."

According to Raul, his son told him of at least 3 incidents in which Nino performed oral sex on Alberto.

The officer asked Raul what Nino told him about Alberto "getting behind him." Raul told the officer that the way Nino described it he believes that Alberto only "dry humped" him outside the clothing. Raul did not believe there was any penetration because Nino never mentioned it or expressed any pain. For that reason Raul never questioned his son any further about it.

Raul told the officer that he spoke to his sister "Sara" (Alberto's mother) about Nino's disclosure. Raul said that Sara is in denial that Alberto did the things that Nino says occurred.

Raul provided the officer with all the contact information for his sister so that the case could be further investigated.

The officer completed his written report and turned it in to his supervisor. The case was sent to the Maricopa County Sheriff's Office Special Victims Unit on June 25, 2006.

Findings of the El Mirage Police Review

This was a very disturbing case involving a 5 year-old boy. This case required further investigation by detectives.

The investigators should have arranged for a forensic interview of the 5 year-old victim. The age of the two boys is certainly a factor to be considered in deciding how the case should be handled within the criminal justice system. If the allegations are true, the 10 year-old cousin's sexual behavior is of great concern. There are clearly physical and emotional issues that will affect both children at their young age.

According to the report, the Special Victims Unit was notified of this incident in June 2006. Based on the information given to the El Mirage Police Department it appears that the sheriff's office did not complete any further work on this case and it was returned to El Mirage in 2007.

There is no information in the Maricopa County Sheriff's report that explains why this case was not worked by their Special Victims Unit.

Very Young Children

Inappropriate sexual activity between _very_ young children is more common than most people think. Oftentimes, these sexual acts (simulated or actual) are completely innocent. However, others may be a sign of a very troubling issue.

Sexual acts by very young children are most always a "learned" behavior. In most cases these children do not understand what they are doing and are simply acting out something they witnessed by adults.

That is why it is important that parents and couples living with young children keep their sexual activity discreet. Parents should also shelter young children from sexually explicit movies.

But, in some cases, sexual activity by a very young child is a response to victimization. Many young children who are victims of sexual abuse will react by performing or attempting to perform sex acts on other children.

This is a very delicate situation and is best handled by a professional. The police should be notified in cases where young children are observed performing or simulating sexual activity. Through effective interview techniques, professional forensic interviewers can normally determine the origin of the child's activity.

****

SECTION THREE

FINAL THOUGHTS

<u>Chapters</u>

14 – Other Mishandled Investigations

15– Leadership and Lessons Learned

Chapter 14

Other Mishandled Investigations

As described earlier, the El Mirage Police Department was a troubled and dysfunctional police department. When the population of El Mirage grew, City Manager B.J. Cornwall wanted to improve police service for their residents. He disbanded the police department and contracted with the local sheriff for police protection.

The Maricopa County Sheriff's Office was paid to provide police service to the City of El Mirage, Arizona for a 2½ year period during 2005 to 2007. Their contract was terminated in October 2007.

In November 2007 I was part of a team that was hired to re-engineer and re-build a "new" El Mirage Police Department. Everyone involved shared a similar vision - a professional police department with a fresh new image.

Throughout this book I have described a host of problems we encountered in dealing with the Maricopa County Sheriff's Office. For reasons I still don't understand, Sheriff Arpaio declared us to be among his "political enemies." Regardless of that, Joe Arpaio's lack of cooperation with the new El Mirage Police Department during the transition period was uncalled for and unprofessional.

The Maricopa County Sheriff's Office knew we had uncovered dozens of sex crime cases they had mishandled while they were in El Mirage. Perhaps Sheriff Arpaio was concerned that the El Mirage Police Department would publicly expose his mishandling of those cases.

The truth is we never intended to expose anything. But, it certainly wasn't due to a lack of scandalous material. Investigators from the "new" El Mirage Police Department uncovered other questionable investigations left behind by the Maricopa County Sheriff's Office.

The Murder of Rachel Rodriguez

Facts of the Case

On June 30, 2005 Rachel Rodriguez was found murdered in her home. The 29 year-old woman mother of three had been shot to death. Family members found the woman's lifeless body inside her bedroom closet.

The victim's boyfriend, Arturo Hernandez Jr., clearly stood out as an investigative lead in the case. On the day she was killed Rodriguez had told her family she was planning to end her stormy relationship with Hernandez. The two had a history of domestic violence and Rodriguez was anxious to move on.

Rodriguez' parents described Hernandez' behavior as "peculiar" on the evening their daughter was killed. Hernandez had called the victim's father and asked him for a ride. He said Rachel was supposed to pick him up but she never showed up. The victim's family said Hernandez' story never added up.

Shortly after Rachel Rodriguez was murdered investigators picked up Hernandez for questioning. The evidence clearly showed he was lying about his whereabouts at the time of the killing. Hernandez' own family members provided investigators with information that contradicted his alibi.

All the evidence pointed to Arturo Hernandez as Rachel Rodriguez' killer but the case was never pursued by the Maricopa County Sheriff's Office.

The El Mirage Police Department Review of the Case

The Maricopa County Sheriff's Office pulled out of El Mirage in late 2007. By that time the unsolved murder case of Rachel Rodriguez was already more than two years old. Rodriguez' case was among dozens of criminal cases left behind by the Maricopa County Sheriff's Office.

As El Mirage investigators examined these cases, the Rachel Rodriguez murder stood out. El Mirage police detectives, supervisors and command staff reviewed the evidence from the initial investigation and concluded the case appeared solvable. In early 2008 the El Mirage investigators re-opened the case.

El Mirage detectives gathered up much of the original information and re-interviewed family members of the victim and suspect. The detectives tracked down Arturo Hernandez who was serving time in an out-of-state prison for an unrelated vehicular manslaughter conviction.

The El Mirage Police detectives travelled to Oklahoma where Hernandez was incarcerated. They interviewed him about the murder of Rachel Rodriguez and obtained a DNA sample. During the interview, Hernandez stuck to his original alibi about his whereabouts at the time Rodriguez was killed.

The detectives knew Hernandez was lying, but now he was locked into that story. The investigators set out to prove he murdered Rachel Rodriguez.

The El Mirage police investigators teamed up with a crime analyst from the Arizona Department of Public Safety. Together they developed a visual timeline that clearly showed Arturo Hernandez killed Rachel Rodriguez.

In December 2009 the El Mirage Police Department presented their evidence to the Maricopa County Attorney's Office. The prosecutor's office agreed that the case looked good and the evidence clearly pointed to Hernandez as the killer.

On April 6, 2010 the El Mirage police took the case before a grand jury and Hernandez was indicted on a 2nd Degree Murder charge in the death of Rachel Rodriguez.

Closure for the Family

Nearly five years after the murder, Rachel Rodriguez and her family finally received justice. Hernandez confessed to killing Rodriguez and pled guilty to 2nd Degree Murder. In July 2010 he was sentenced to 10 years in prison for the murder.

The frustration and grief of Rachel Rodriguez' family came to a head during Hernandez's sentencing hearing. The family was present to testify and ask the judge for the maximum sentence. As the shackled Hernandez was escorted into the courtroom Rachel Rodriguez' 17 year-old son "sucker punched" him in the face.

All the evidence used by the El Mirage Police Department to arrest and convict Arturo Hernandez was available to the Maricopa County Sheriff's Office in 2005. Hernandez had motive, means and opportunity to commit the murder of Rachel Rodriguez. When the murder first occurred the evidence was "fresh" and all the Maricopa County Sheriff's Office had to do was connect the dots.

For five long years the children and other family members of Rachel Rodriquez were left to wonder if her killer would ever be caught. Sadly, this murder case could have been solved and the killer arrested within a few days of her death.

The Shooting Death of Jose Luis Calderon Chagoya

Jose Calderon Chagoya – "Suicide" - August 5, 2005

Around noon on August 5, 2005, three Hispanic men went to a home located on north Honcho Street in El Mirage looking for 22 year-old Jose Luis Calderon Chagoya. The men knocked on the door and Chagoya's pregnant girlfriend answered. She told the men that Chagoya was not home but would be back soon. The men insisted on seeing Chagoya and asked her to call them when he got home. The three then drove away in a white van.

About an hour later Chagoya returned home and his girlfriend told him about the three visitors. A few minutes later the trio returned and Chagoya went outside to talk with the men. Moments later the girlfriend heard a single gunshot and ran outside. She found Chagoya lying on the ground bleeding from a gunshot wound to the head. A revolver was lying on the ground next to him – on his left side.

Chagoya's girlfriend said she saw the three men running away as she came out after hearing the gunshot. She said they returned a few moments later and sped off in the white van.

The police and Fire Department received several 911 calls about the incident and responded quickly to the location. Paramedics treated Chagoya at the scene but he died shortly after arrival at a Phoenix hospital.

Chagoya's girlfriend told investigators that she had seen the three men before and believed they were acquaintances of Chagoya. She said she only knew the three men by their nicknames.

The officers and deputies who responded to the scene concluded it was a homicide. The three men had been looking for Chagoya earlier in the day and returned after he got home. According to his girlfriend they were outside with Chagoya when he was shot and all three fled the scene.

Homicide detectives from the Maricopa County Sheriff's Office responded to take over the investigation. The incident was treated as a homicide and the crime scene was processed and photographed. The gun used to shoot Chagoya was impounded as evidence.

The investigators gathered as much information as they could from Chagoya's girlfriend about the three men who were present when Chagoya was shot. Officers and deputies were alerted to search for the three men.

Weeks later one of the three men was identified and located. He was brought in for questioning by Maricopa County Sheriff's detectives. The man admitted he was present when Chagoya was shot, but said that Chagoya *shot himself*. He claimed that Chagoya was playing *Russian roulette* with a revolver and shot himself. The man said he and his friends got scared and ran from the scene.

Apparently, this was all the Maricopa County Sheriff's investigators needed to hear. They took the man's word and no charges were ever filed. No further investigation was conducted. The detectives declared the shooting a *"suicide"* and Exceptionally Cleared the case.

I suppose the suicide conclusion is plausible. But the case leaves many unanswered questions in the mind of an experienced homicide investigator.

- Why was the gun found on the victim's left side if he was right-handed?
- Was the gun checked for Chagoya's fingerprints or DNA
- Why did the three men flee the scene? Witnessing a "friend" shoot himself in the head is a traumatic event. Innocent witnesses usually don't flee.

- If they were innocent, why didn't the three men come forward later?
- Why weren't the other two men tracked down and interviewed?

This was a shooting death that clearly warranted more investigation.

The Stabbing Death of Robert Johnson

Robert Johnson – "Suicide" – October 19, 2005

On October 19, 2005, 49 year-old Robert Johnson and his wife were embroiled in a domestic dispute. The couple had a long history of visits from the police about domestic violence incidents.

On this particular day, Johnson's wife said they were fighting and he was chasing her around the house. She said she threw a salt & pepper shaker at him trying to get away. The wife said she left the house and drove away to let Johnson cool off.

She claimed she returned home a short while later and found her husband lying in the driveway with multiple stab wounds to his chest. Johnson later died of his injuries – *11 stab wounds to the chest*.

Johnson's wife was interrogated by detectives but she denied stabbing him. Officers found the blood-stained knife several yards from Johnson's body on a sidewalk leading to the front door of the home.

A neighbor witnessed part of the dispute from her kitchen window, but did not see the actual stabbing. What the witness told investigators was not consistent with Johnson's wife's version of what happened.

During her interview with detectives, Johnson's wife stuck hard and fast to her story that she did not stab her husband. She admitted they were fighting, but insisted she left the house before the stabbing occurred.

Apparently, the Maricopa County Sheriff's detectives believed Mrs. Johnson's story and let her go. The Maricopa County Sheriff's Office ruled the death a *"suicide"* and no charges were ever filed against her.

Some El Mirage officers said they later learned that Johnson's wife received a sizable payoff from her late husband's life insurance policy and moved out of state.

The idea that Robert Johnson's death was a suicide is *"possible."* But, just like the other cases, this one leaves some issues unaddressed.

- The autopsy revealed Johnson suffered 11 stab wounds to the chest, three of which were *fatal* wounds. Multiple stab wounds to a victim typically indicates a crime of incredible anger or rage.

- Is it even *possible* for a person to stab themselves 11 times? After just a few painful stab wounds the human body would go into shock. And three of Johnson's stab wounds were declared to be *fatal wounds* by the medical examiner.
- Is a suicidal man going to *stab* himself? As morbid as it sounds, death by stabbing is a slow and painful way to die.
- How did the bloody knife end up yards away from the victim near the front door of the house?
- The witness's statements were not consistent with Mrs. Johnson's account of what happened that day.

The Johnson couple had a long history of domestic violence. The police had responded numerous times to their home. Mrs. Johnson had motive, means and opportunity to kill her husband.

The only thing that remains a mystery about this case is *how* the Maricopa County Sheriff's Office declared this death a *suicide*.

The Rachel Rodriguez, Jose Chagoya and Robert Johnson cases highlight yet another problem within Sheriff Joe Arpaio's organization. Unfortunately, I could list at least five other cases that are equally questionable.

In the next chapter I discuss leadership and the traits of effective leaders. Good leaders accept *personal* responsibility for mistakes made by their organization. Because of his unquenchable thirst for good press, Sheriff Joe Arpaio doesn't admit personal responsibility for shortcomings. And, never hesitates to put his chief deputy out front to take the hits.

****

Chapter 15

Leadership and Lessons Learned

I had the honor to serve under one of the greatest military leaders in the history of the United States Army - Harold "Hal" Moore. I never served with him in combat but was under his command in Bravo Company, 4th Battalion, 1st Infantry Brigade at Fort Ord, California.

The leadership skills of Lieutenant Colonel Moore were depicted in the 2002 film *"We Were Soldiers."* Actor Mel Gibson portrayed the charismatic Moore who served in World War II, Korea and Vietnam.

The movie tells the story of how Col. Moore and his crusty assistant, Sergeant Major Basil Plumley, developed the Army's first air assault battalion. In 1964 Col. Moore was given command of the 2nd Battalion, 23rd Infantry, 11th Air Assault Division at Fort Benning, Georgia. When the 11th Air Assault Division was inactivated in 1965, his battalion was re-designated the 1st Battalion, 7th Cavalry Regiment, 1st Cavalry Division (the now-infamous Air Mobile or Air Cavalry).

Anyone who served in the U.S. Army or is a military buff knows the rest of this story. In August 1965, Col. Moore and his 1st Cavalry Division were deployed to Vietnam. In November the battalion attacked and decisively defeated a North Vietnamese regiment in the historic battle at Ia Drang Valley. The tremendous leadership skills of Hal Moore, Basil Plumley and others were a major factor in the victory.

The leadership styles of Col. Moore and Sergeant Major Plumley were as opposite as day and night. Moore was caring, compassionate and amazingly decisive under fire. Plumley was a tall, intimidating and gruff-looking combat veteran. Yet they were both effective leaders and instilled confidence in their soldiers by their mere presence.

The highly decorated Harold "Hal" Moore retired from the U.S. Army in 1977 as a Lieutenant General. He has remained active in volunteer work and many activities. A highly spiritual man, General "Hal" Moore has authored several books about his experiences in war and peacetime.

There are many other films that depict different leadership skills. Many are traditional war movies where someone usually emerges as a hero.

But, diverse leadership styles in corporate, family or disaster settings have also been illustrated in other great films. The characters in movies such as *"Wall Street,"* *"The Help"* and *"Titanic"* can all be used to study different personalities and leadership styles.

Great Leaders

Leadership is an intangible quality. Simply put, leadership is the effective application of experience, courage and character. It is also a set of skills – communication, competency and compassion. A good leader is *aware* of each of these traits. A great leader *applies* all of them.

As described above, U.S. Army General Hal Moore was a great military leader. His real-life leadership skills were demonstrated in a popular war movie.

Some of the better leadership training classes I attended have incorporated the study of characters portrayed in other famous war films. The movie *"Twelve O'clock High"* illustrates a variety of leadership styles in several different military officers and enlisted men. It is interesting to watch the stronger leaders in the movie and observe how others respond to them.

The character played by Tom Selleck in the TV police drama *"Blue Bloods"* represents one of the best leaders of a police department. In the show, NYPD Police Commissioner *Frank Reagan* is the epitome of a great police leader. He accepts responsibility when mistakes are made by the people in his organization, and he takes immediate and decisive steps to correct them. He reaches out to those who were wronged and tries to make it right. He praises his people, not himself, for the successes made by his organization.

There truly is a common thread among great leaders. Most of them espouse to the same time-tested traits and characteristics. They display courage under fire, use effective communication skills and show compassion for their people. They each accept responsibility for their own actions and those of their subordinates.

Poor Leadership

A person's "character" also plays a role in their effectiveness as a leader. Their integrity and compassion are subconsciously applied to their strategic (long-term) and tactical (immediate) decision-making.

A person in a leadership role who lacks compassion for people is rarely viewed as an "effective" leader. They are generally seen as someone more interested in their own personal achievement - at the cost of others. In high-risk occupations such as the military, police or fire services, they are rarely seen on the front lines, often demand protection and generally remain rear echelon.

A person of questionable integrity is generally not trusted by their subordinates. That person will often shift blame to others and misrepresent facts in order to shield themselves from criticism. They often are viewed as a "bully" because they exploit their leadership "position" for personal gain.

Ineffective leaders generally struggle with decision making. Quite often they are so worried about "looking bad" or making a mistake that they paralyze progress with their indecision. Under enemy fire is not a good time to form a committee to make a decision. There is some truth to the adage, "a bad decision is better than no decision at all."

Position Power vs. People Power

Leadership positions inherently include authority and power. Through training and personal experience I have learned there are two types of leadership power – *position* power and *people* power. They are different but not necessarily mutually exclusive of each other.

By virtue of their "job title" most managers are granted *"position power."* This is the authority vested in them by their rank or management title. Like it or not, we are obligated by rules or policies to follow their direction.

On the other hand, *"people power"* is the true measure of an effective leader. It occurs when the leader is empowered by their *subordinates* through respect, trust and confidence.

Many people in leadership roles are granted *"position power"* but never seem to acquire *"people power."*

Management vs. Leadership

Management and leadership are often taught as a combined topic of instruction. Management is often defined as *getting things done through other people.* Leadership is *the ability to influence others to accomplish a goal.*

While there are similarities in their definitions, there are distinctions which separate them. Many people are able to promote to management positions but never become effective leaders.

Countless books have been written on the subject of leadership. Many different people have marketed their "leadership tools" programs. Service industries and corporations often purchase these programs in an effort to build strong leaders within their organization.

Companies and government entities invest millions of dollars each year trying to develop their managers into leaders. Bosses understand the value of effective leadership. Goals will more likely be achieved under the direction and guidance of good leaders.

Leadership Training

During my career with the Phoenix Police Department it seemed like we adopted a new "leadership philosophy" every few years. We usually joked about each new leadership training program as the "flavor of the month."

Here's how it usually worked. Police management would *compel* all supervisors and commanders to attend the training session. The creator of the new flavor would try to sell us a bill of goods that his training philosophy would revolutionize our police department. Most of them promised to "empower" everyone in the organization into the role of a great leader.

Those of us who had been leaders in the organization for any length of time knew it was all nonsense. But, it was mandatory "training" and we sat through it.

It wasn't the concept of "leadership" training that we considered nonsense. *Great leadership equates to effective organizations* - that part rings true. But, the notion that their product was better than anyone else's flavor of leadership training was only a sales pitch.

The basic tenets of leadership remain constant. The U.S. military cornered the market on leadership training eons ago. One of the best leadership training philosophies of all times is still the West Point Leadership model.

Police departments and other organizations could save millions of dollars in training costs by adopting a *single* leadership training model. Over time they would develop a cadre of effective leaders who espouse to a standard leadership style.

Leadership in Law Enforcement

Everyone assumes a leadership role at some time in their life. It may be in a family environment as a parent, in a church setting or at work. And in that role we often experience the challenges associated with leadership.

Running an effective law enforcement organization is all about leadership and character. After 38 years of military and police service I have learned a thing or two about leadership.

I have had the privilege of working alongside some great leaders in my Army and police careers. But, I also gained valuable insight from several very poor leaders as well. I watched how they functioned and vowed never to be that kind of leader.

But, much of this book has been about Sheriff Joe Arpaio and the manner in which he runs the Maricopa County Sheriff's Office. So, I would be remiss if I didn't share my opinions about his "leadership" in running a law enforcement agency.

Sheriff Joe Arpaio has made himself popular among some voters in Maricopa County. Outside of his organization he has created a persona that is mostly smoke and mirrors.

The real test of leadership comes from *within* the organization. In my opinion, Sheriff Joe Arpaio fails to display any true leadership skills. His management style appears contrary to nearly every principle of modern law enforcement leadership training.

It is no secret that Sheriff Arpaio runs his organization through fear and intimidation. He rewards blind loyalty and doesn't tolerate a differing opinion. Favoritism is a means to job assignments and promotions. I had heard this first hand from several employees of the sheriff's office. Then it was confirmed in an internal memo written by one of Sheriff Arpaio's own higher-ups. In 2010, Maricopa County Sheriff's Deputy Chief Frank Munnell wrote a 63-page memo about the internal workings of the Maricopa County Sheriff's Office. That revealing memo launched a series of investigations about how the sheriff runs his office.

Anyone who reads the paper or watches the TV news in Arizona knows Sheriff Arpaio routinely denies knowledge of shortcomings and defers blame to others within his organization when mistakes are exposed. That is truly unfortunate for the many fine men and women who currently work at the Maricopa County Sheriff's Office.

Lessons Learned

The Mishandled Sex Crimes Investigations

During my three years as the Assistant Police Chief in El Mirage we had *many* internal conversations about the scandalous level of negligence on the part of the Maricopa County Sheriff's Office. We often asked ourselves how such wide spread neglect of serious criminal investigations could happen?

We sought answers to this and other questions about the performance of the Maricopa County Sheriff's Office in El Mirage. Within a few months we figured out what happened as we cleaned up the messes they left behind.

The dozens of neglected sex-crimes cases of children were the most disturbing to all of us. We figured out that these cases were left untouched due to staffing levels and manpower decisions made by Sheriff Arpaio and his top aides.

In years passed I had worked with some of the detectives assigned to the Maricopa County Sheriff's Special Victims Unit. They were dedicated law enforcement officers. They would *never* have intentionally let these victims go without justice being served. Something had influenced their ability to do their jobs effectively.

As we probed deeper we learned that part of the problem was the staffing level of the Special Victims Unit. Manpower had been decimated and the few remaining detectives were forced to handle an unreasonable number of cases.

The sheriff was reassigning *detectives* to politically motivated assignments like immigration enforcement, his Anti-Smuggling Unit and Conspiracy Squads.

For a while the Special Victims Unit had as few as four detectives to handle sex crime cases for the entire county. Investigative supervisors reportedly warned their chain of command that the detectives could not keep up with the backlog of cases.

As Sheriff Arpaio depleted his investigative units to conduct "immigration sweeps," dozens of serious criminal investigations were neglected. While his beefed-up Conspiracy Squad was out chasing ghosts, the sex-crime victims of El Mirage were neglected. Serious criminal investigations were overlooked while Joe Arpaio was out rounding up landscapers and dishwashers.

This situation in its totality clearly demonstrates why local police or sheriff's departments should *never* make immigration their primary enforcement goal. Their primary responsibility is to protect their residents and enforce local laws.

Manpower Allocation

Former Phoenix City Manager Frank Fairbanks once spoke at a training seminar I attended. He gave us a pearl of wisdom that I remember to this day. He said, _"Give your employees the opportunity to do a good job. Provide them with the time and resources they need - and they will be successful."_

As a long-time police commander in a major police force I fully understand the concepts of organizational goals and manpower allocation. At the Phoenix Police Department I managed and worked some of the most complex murder, organized crime and conspiracy cases in Phoenix history.

Management must adequately staff its investigative units in order for detectives to keep up with the workload. Without adequate resources cases will be neglected.

There are two important keys to effective police management.

- _Prioritize_ crime suppression goals.
- Allocate personnel resources effectively.

It appears that the Maricopa County Sheriff's Office was ineffective in both areas. Sheriff Arpaio made _immigration enforcement_ a top priority for his deputies. And in doing so, he depleted manpower resources from important investigative units like the Special Victims Unit.

Organizational Failure

The Maricopa County Sheriff's Office failed to properly investigate dozens, perhaps hundreds, of sex crimes. What happened in El Mirage was not just mistakes made by individuals within the Special Victims Unit - it was an *organizational failure*.

The negligence that occurred in El Mirage points to a systemic problem in Sheriff Arpaio's office. The failure started with Joe Arpaio himself and his misaligned enforcement priorities.

Sheriff Arpaio lost sight of the fact that his primary mission is to provide police service to the residents of Maricopa County and contract cities. Instead, he focused on gimmicks and fanfare about "immigration enforcement" that did virtually nothing to prevent violent crime in his jurisdiction.

Defining Moments

Andrew Thomas was the Maricopa County Attorney from January 2005 until he resigned in April 2010. During that time Thomas and Sheriff Joe Arpaio launched a series of baseless investigations against Arpaio's "political enemies." In early 2012, Andrew Thomas was brought up on ethics and other charges for his part in those investigations. On April 10, 2012 a panel from the Arizona Supreme Court found "clear and convincing evidence" in support of the charges. Andrew Thomas was disbarred and stripped of license to practice law.

What happens to Sheriff Joe Arpaio for his part in these schemes remains to be seen. As of today, the United States Department of Justice has on-going criminal and civil investigations covering a wide variety of activities and practices of Sheriff Arpaio and his organization.

Certain events or twists of fate often create defining moments in our lives. Perhaps this will be one of those moments for Maricopa County Sheriff Joe Arpaio.

Final Thoughts

I often mentioned to Chief Frazier that the public had a right to know what happened in El Mirage. But, I also knew that *professional courtesy* among law enforcement agencies would preclude us from exposing the negligence of the Maricopa County Sheriff's Office. So, we notified Sheriff Arpaio but never leaked it to the media.

Sheriff Joe Arpaio has ruled as a tyrant for many years. Employees of the Maricopa County Sheriff's Office have worked in an environment of intimidation and fear – not from the dangers of police work on the street – but from the head of the organization.

Many employees have endured Arpaio's tyranny in silence. Speaking out would subject them to intimidation, bullying, transfers or worse. Many have families to support and aren't willing to risk losing their job. So, many have kept their mouths shut and quietly gone about their business.

The details in this book are only a *trickle* of information about the Maricopa County Sheriff's Office under Joe Arpaio. When he is finally voted out of office employees will no longer feel their jobs are in jeopardy. At that point I believe the *floodgates* of truth about Joe Arpaio will open wide.

Somebody once said *'the world is a classroom and life is our teacher.'* I believe the context of that quote implies that our ability to learn goes far beyond the education we get in school. Exposure to reality can be a powerful lesson.

Early in my police career my mentor gave me some great advice. He said, *"Anyone can make a mistake. What matters is what you do next."* Apparently, Joe Arpaio was never taught to take ownership of mistakes – that it builds character.

I have concluded that Sheriff Joe Arpaio learned *nothing* from the disgraceful sex-crime scandal that so severely blemished his reputation. In fact, he refused to accept any personal blame from this failure. The problem is, you can't run from the truth.

And the most distasteful thing of all was Sheriff Arpaio's refusal to even *acknowledge* the victims who suffered a tremendous injustice on his watch as sheriff of Maricopa County.

I raised my children in an environment where it was OK to disagree with people. They were taught that disagreement was considered healthy and helped both parties grow. Vindictiveness and bullying were never part of my family's response to a differing opinion.

Joe Arpaio often referred to me as his "political enemy." I am not an enemy of anyone in law enforcement. I dedicated most of my adult life to serving my community as a police officer. It is shameful for him to publicly refer to me in this manner simply because I have a differing opinion.

It seems to me that Joe Arpaio lost sight of his true responsibility as sheriff and became more engrained in publicity rather than doing the right thing.

Just ask the victims...

"If There Were Any Victims"

Glossary of Terms

A.Z.P.O.S.T. – The acronym for the Arizona Peace Officers Standards and Training Board. This Arizona state board regulates "sworn" police officers and deputies of all ranks. The board establishes hiring, training and retention standards for all city, state and county law enforcement officers in Arizona.

CASE MANAGEMENT – This term describes a system that a law enforcement agency uses to effectively manage a detective's workload. Typically, a case management system tracks how many cases a detective is assigned and how long the detective has been working each case. The system also includes a current "status" of each open case. Case Management is used by the detective's supervisor to monitor the detective's workload and productivity.

CHAIN OF COMMAND – Describes the order in which authority and power in an organization is wielded and delegated. This term is widely used in military and paramilitary organizations. In its strictest sense employees report only to their immediate supervisor. Orders and directions are typically given downward along the chain of command with results and accountability flowing upward.

CHAIN OF CUSTODY - The "chain of custody" is an important legal term that deals with evidence of a crime and who handled it. The term refers to the chronological documentation of evidence from the moment the evidence is seized by the police at a crime scene until it is presented in court. During a trial, prosecutors have to account for every person who handled that piece of evidence. This strict accountability process is critical to maintain the integrity of the evidence.

CHIEF DEPUTY – Refers to the title (rank) of the second highest ranking sworn officer in the sheriff's office – also known as the Second in Command.

COLOR OF AUTHORITY – Describes the term which gives police officers the power to take certain actions. Color of Authority means actions under the law, typically on-duty. Gives the lawful right to take certain actions.

CONFRONTATION CALL – This is an investigative strategy of tape-recording a telephone conversation between a victim and suspect. A detective will typically coach the victim on what to say before placing the call. Once on the phone, the victim immediately confronts the suspect about the crime he or she committed. Typically, the element of surprise will cause the suspect to make incriminating statements if they are "guilty." If guilty, a suspect will often panic during a confrontation call and make incriminating statements. If an accused person is innocent, they typically display a whole different set of responses to the allegation. Confrontation calls are very effective tools used by law enforcement in "he said, she said" sex crimes where there are no independent witnesses.

COUNTY ATTORNEY – In the state of Arizona, a County Attorney is the "prosecutor" and represents the "state" in criminal trials in Superior Court (felonies) and Justice Court (misdemeanors). Each Arizona county has an elected County Attorney whose office is responsible for prosecuting felonies and certain other local cases within their respective county. In other states, the prosecutors are also know an as the "State's Attorney" or "District Attorney."

DEPUTY – refers to the title (rank) of the line-level member of a sheriff's department. Deputies are sworn employees.

DEPUTY CHIEF – refers to the title (rank) of an executive level member of a sheriff's office and some police departments. Some police agencies refer to this rank as Assistant Chief.

DUE PROCESS - Due process is the legal requirement of government to respect the legal rights of an accused person. Due process is designed to ensure a person is treated fairly and protect them from violations of their constitutional rights.

FELONY – A serious crime that carries a sentence of incarceration (one year or longer) in the Arizona Department of Corrections (state prison).

FIRST RESPONDER - The "first responders" are typically the uniformed officers and deputies you routinely see driving around in "marked" police cruisers. These are the officers who respond when you call 911 or the police for help. They drive fully marked police cars and are in full uniform so they are clearly recognized as the police when they arrive on the scene of an emergency.

FOLLOW-UP - The term "follow-up" is used in a broad sense as it pertains to detectives. Follow-up by detectives can include a host of activities and investigative strategies. Depending on the type of crime, those activities might include: an in-depth interview of the victim; interviews with witnesses, relatives and neighbors; a search warrant to collect evidence; identifying and locating the suspect; and arresting and interrogating the suspect.

FORENSIC EXAMINATION – A physical examination of a location, article or person with the purpose of locating and seizing scientific, physical or trace (microscopic) evidence. A forensic examination normally refers to the search for DNA, blood, hair and body fluids.

FORENSIC INTERVIEW - A forensic interview is typically conducted in a non-threatening environment at a location such as the Child Help facility in Phoenix or the Family Advocacy Center in Glendale, Arizona. This type of interview is conducted by a specially trained child counselor who is normally considered an expert in the field of child victims. At the conclusion of a forensic interview the examiner can typically make a recommendation as to whether the child victim is telling the truth. Forensic interviews are generally mandated by the prosecutor's office before they will ever proceed with a case in court.

JURISDICTION - Jurisdiction is the term used to describe an entity's "authority" over a certain area or certain persons. In the criminal justice system in Arizona jurisdiction typically refers to a particular geographic area where a police agency or criminal court has legal authority to perform their duties.

MARICOPA COUNTY - Maricopa County, Arizona is located in the central part of the state of Arizona. It is named after a proud, indigenous Native American group from the region. Maricopa County includes the metro-Phoenix area and has a population of over 4,000,000 people.

MISDEMEANOR – A lesser crime that carries a penalty of a fine and/or sentence (up to one year) to incarceration in a county jail.

N.C.I.C. (National Crime Information Center) - is a computerized database of criminal justice information. It includes data on wanted persons, fugitives, stolen vehicles and property, missing persons and criminal history information on individuals. Access to the information is restricted to law enforcement and criminal justice agencies. The data is accessible 24 hours a day, 365 days a year.

NON-SWORN OR CIVILIAN EMPLOYEES - The "civilian" or non-sworn employees are generally the professional support staff. Non-sworn employees fulfill important positions from entry level-file clerks to executive-level managers.

PEACE OFFICER – another term for police officer or deputy.

SPECIAL VICTIMS UNIT – The unit within the Maricopa County Sheriff's Office that investigates sex crimes.

SEARCH WARRANT – A written order issued by a court, pursuant to the sworn affidavit of a law enforcement officer, attesting that probable cause exists that a crime is being, or has been committed, at a specific location, and that evidence of that crime is presently at that location. The search warrant authorizes law enforcement officers to lawfully enter the premises and seize evidence specified in the search warrant.

SWORN EMPLOYEE – "Sworn" employees are the police officers and deputies of all ranks. They have taken a special oath of office to uphold the law and uphold the United States Constitution.

ABOUT THE AUTHOR

William C. "Bill" Louis grew up in Phoenix, Arizona and graduated from Brophy College Prep. After honorably serving in the United States Army he returned to Phoenix where he and his wife raised their family. Bill chose a career in law enforcement spending nearly 31 years with the Phoenix Police Department rising through the ranks to Assistant Police Chief.

During his law enforcement career, Assistant Chief Louis gained a wide range of experience through assignments in Patrol, Training, Organized Crime, Vice, Crimes Against Children, Internal Affairs, Violent Crimes (homicide, robbery and assaults) and Homeland Security. Assistant Chief Louis led the successful task force investigations for two Phoenix, Arizona serial murder investigations known as the *Baseline Killer* and *Serial Shooter* cases.

He was responsible for other high profile investigations of Asian Organized Crime, the Russian Mafia, the Hell's Angels and the Mexican Mafia. Chief Louis also headed up Phoenix police security planning and operations for the 2001 World Series and the 2008 Super Bowl. Following the events of September 11, 2001, Chief Louis was assigned to the FBI's Joint Terrorism Task Force and remained there until his retirement from law enforcement. Due to the sensitive nature of some of his assignments, Chief Louis held a Top Secret Security clearance through the FBI.

After 31 years with the Phoenix Police Department, Assistant Chief Louis was hired by the City of El Mirage, Arizona in 2007 to help re-build and re-engineer their police department. He spent the next three years implementing new policies, developing new enforcement strategies and promoting community involvement in the police department.

Assistant Chief Louis was in charge of the El Mirage investigative team that uncovered the criminal investigations mishandled by the Maricopa County Sheriff's Office. Their team spent more than 12 months reviewing and re-investigating the child sex crimes and death investigations that Sheriff Joe Arpaio's agency neglected.

Throughout his 34 years in law enforcement Assistant Chief Louis was active in many organizations including the International Police Association, International Association of Chiefs of Police, the Arizona Chiefs Association, the Association of Former Army Security Agents and the Association of Former Intelligence Officers.

Chief Louis retired from law enforcement in 2010. He lives with his wife in Peoria, Arizona where he remains active in his community. Chief Louis is an accomplished guitar player and plays in a light-rock band. His other interests include travel, scuba diving, wood work and spending time with his grandchildren.

Chief Louis is fluent in the German language. He holds a Bachelor's Degree from the University of Phoenix and a Master's Degree in Education from Northern Arizona University.

Made in the USA
San Bernardino, CA
21 June 2016